W9-AKE-241

Raccoons

and Their Relatives

Concept and Product Development: Editorial Options, Inc.
Series Designer: Karen Donica
Book Author: Pat Harvey Sullivan

For information on other World Book
products, visit us at our Web site at
http://www.worldbook.com

For information on sales to schools and libraries
in the United States, call 1-800-975-3250.

For information on sales to schools and libraries
in Canada, call 1-800-837-5365.

World Book, Inc.
233 N. Michigan Avenue
Chicago, IL 60601

Library of Congress Cataloging-in-Publication Data

Sullivan, Pat Harvey.
    Raccoons and their relatives.
      p. cm. -- (World Book's animals of the world)
    Summary: Provides information about the physical characteristics, habits, and behavior
    of raccoons and such related species as the coati, kinkajou, red panda, and ringtail.
    ISBN 0-7166-1228-3 -- ISBN 0-7166-1223-2 (set)
    1. Raccoons--Juvenile literature. 2. Procyonidae--Juvenile literature. [1. Raccoons. 2.
Procyonids.] I. Title. II. Series.
    QL737.C26 S85 2002
    599.76'3--dc21   2001046712

Printed in Malaysia

1 2 3 4 5 6 7 8 9 06 05 04 03 02

Picture Acknowledgments: Cover: © Ron Sanford, Photo Researchers; © François Gohier, Photo Researchers; © Thomas
Kitchin, Tom Stack & Associates; © Joe McDonald, Bruce Coleman Collection; © Patricio Robles Gil, Bruce Coleman Inc.

© Erwin & Peggy Bauer, Bruce Coleman Collection 11; © Erwin & Peggy Bauer, Bruce Coleman Inc. 27; © Erwin & Peggy Bauer,
Animals Animals 43; © Paul Berquist, Animals Animals 31; © Tom Brakefield, Bruce Coleman Inc. 35.; © Janis Burger, Bruce
Coleman Inc. 53; © Alan & Sandy Carey, Photo Researchers 51; © Stephen Dalton, Photo Researchers 5; © Tim Davis, Photo
Researchers 5, 57; © François Gohier, Photo Researchers 23, 41; © Thomas Kitchin, Tom Stack & Associates 37, 39;
© C. C. Lockwood, Bruce Coleman Inc. 25; © Steve Maslowski, Photo Researchers 17, 29; © Joe McDonald, Animals Animals
15; © Joe McDonald, Bruce Coleman Collection 55; © Joe McDonald, Bruce Coleman Inc. 19, 33; © Patti Murray, Animals
Animals 47; © Leonide Principe, Photo Researchers 45; © Patricio Robles Gil, Bruce Coleman Inc. 49; © Leonard Lee Rue III,
Bruce Coleman Inc. 21; © Ron Stanford, Photo Researchers 4, 7; © Rod Williams, Bruce Coleman Inc. 61.

Illustrations: WORLD BOOK illustration by Kersti Mack 9, 62; WORLD BOOK illustration by Michael DiGiorgio 13.

World Book's Animals of the World

Raccoons
and Their Relatives

Doesn't anyone want to hang out with me?

World Book, Inc.
A Scott Fetzer Company
Chicago

Contents

Do I hide behind a mask?

What do I like to do when I hang out?

Am I all thumbs?

What Are Raccoons and Their Relatives?

You probably know what raccoons are. You may even have seen raccoons in your own backyard. But do you know what cacomistles *(KAK uh MIHS uhlz)* are? How about coatis *(koh AH teez)* or kinkajous *(KINK kuh jooz)*?

The raccoon you see here is a northern raccoon. It belongs to a family of animals called *procyonids (proh SY uh nihdz)*. Cacomistles, coatis, and kinkajous are also in this family. So are ringtails and red pandas.

Raccoons and their relatives are carnivores *(KAHR nuh vawrz),* or meat eaters. Carnivores have large canine teeth and four or five toes on each foot. Cats, dogs, and bears are other examples of carnivores. Raccoons and their relatives are also mammals. Mammals are warm-blooded animals that have hair or fur on their bodies. And mammal mothers nurse their young using their own milk.

Northern raccoon

Where in the World Do These Animals Live?

There are two main species, or kinds, of raccoons. One is the northern raccoon. The other is the crab-eating raccoon. The northern raccoon lives in Canada, the United States, Mexico, and Central America. The crab-eating raccoon lives in parts of Central and South America and on some nearby islands.

Some other species of raccoons live on tropical islands in the Americas. For example, the Cozumel *(KAHZ uh muhl)* Island raccoon lives on the Mexican island of Cozumel.

All other raccoon relatives, except for the red panda, also live in the Americas. The red panda lives in Asia.

About 60 years ago, people took raccoons to Europe and Asia to keep in zoos or on preserves. They also bred raccoons for their fur. Some of the animals were released. Others escaped. As a result, raccoons can now also be found in very small areas in Europe and Asia.

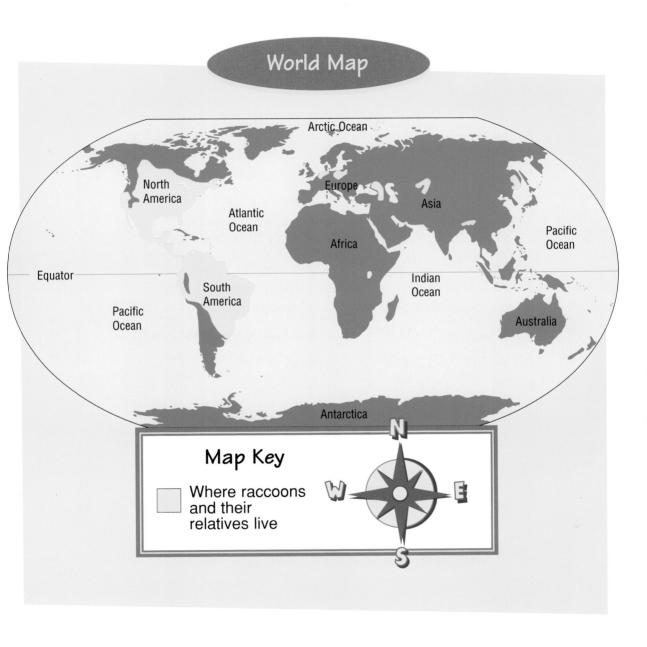

World Map

Arctic Ocean

North America

Europe

Asia

Atlantic Ocean

Africa

Pacific Ocean

Equator

South America

Indian Ocean

Pacific Ocean

Australia

Antarctica

Map Key

Where raccoons and their relatives live

N

W E

S

Do Raccoons Wear Masks?

Raccoons don't wear masks, but, as you can see in the picture, it sure looks as if they do. Raccoons have wide patches of black fur around their eyes and across their cheeks. This striking pattern looks just like a bandit's black mask!

A raccoon has other markings that make it easy to identify, too. Its long, bushy tail has 5 to 10 black rings around it. The tip of the tail is dark in color. Like a grizzly bear's fur, a raccoon's fur is grizzled, or streaked with gray. It also has flecks of yellow or brown in it. Raccoon fur is long and coarse. Thick fur makes a raccoon look bigger than it really is.

"Masked" raccoons

What's Under a Raccoon's Fur?

The rest of the raccoon, of course! Here you see a diagram of the skeleton, or bones, of a northern raccoon.

A raccoon's head is shaped like that of a fox. It is wide at the forehead and narrows to a pointed snout. A raccoon has 40 teeth—including four long, sharp canines.

A raccoon's legs are fairly long for its body size. Each foot has five toes. The toes are so long that they are often called fingers. At the end of each finger is a long, sharp claw. A raccoon walks on the soles of its feet, just as a bear does.

All raccoons share similar features, but they're not all the same size. Northern raccoons are the biggest raccoons. They are about 24 to 42 inches (61 to 107 centimeters) long and weigh from 8 to 20 pounds (3.6 to 9 kilograms). Male raccoons are usually bigger than females.

Raccoon Skeleton

Snout

Canines

Claws

Toes

13

What's Special About a Raccoon's "Hands"?

A raccoon's fingers are long and flexible. The fingers are also spaced far apart. With "hands" like these, a raccoon can hold things almost as well as a monkey can.

A raccoon's hands are seldom still. The raccoon uses the fingers of its forepaws to feel around. As it feels around, it sometimes finds food. That's how a raccoon can catch fish without even looking. A raccoon often stares straight ahead as it puts its hands into the water. It holds its hands there until it feels something move. Then the raccoon grabs its catch and brings it to its nose. After a quick smell, the raccoon pops its catch into its mouth.

At the end of a raccoon's fingers are strong claws. These help the raccoon grasp or climb just about anything, from a garbage can to a tree. This climbing ability comes in handy when the raccoon wants to find food or escape from enemies.

Raccoon using its "hands"

Are Raccoons Fussy Eaters?

Not at all! Raccoons are happy to dine on a wide variety of foods. Although they are carnivores, they will eat plants as well as meat. In fact, they will eat just about anything they can find.

While raccoons are not fussy eaters, they find their favorite foods in or near the water. Raccoons love fish, crayfish, crabs, frogs, and other freshwater animals. But they also like fruits, nuts, seeds, bird eggs, grasshoppers, and small animals such as mice.

Raccoons are also scavengers. That means that they will eat what humans or other animals leave behind. The raccoons you see here are dining on some tasty snacks from a tipped over garbage can!

Raccoons scavenging

Do Raccoons Wash Their Food?

No, probably not. But raccoons do have an unusual habit. They often dunk food into water before eating it!

The scientific name for the northern raccoon is *procyon lotor (PROH see ahn LOH tuhr),* which means "washing bear." It is easy to see how the raccoon got this name. A raccoon's fur looks a lot like that of a grizzly bear, and a raccoon often seems to wash its food.

Scientists once wondered if raccoons really washed their food. So they watched raccoons in captivity. The animals did dunk their food into water—if there was water around. But even if there was no water, the animals still went through the same dunking motions. The scientists concluded that the raccoons were just imitating something they did in the wild when they fished for food.

18

Raccoon dunking food

Where Is a Raccoon's Home?

A raccoon's home, or den, can be almost anywhere. Raccoons don't usually build their own dens, however. They look for empty places to hide away—and just move right in.

Raccoons that live in forests look for hollow spaces in tree trunks. If there is a pond or a stream nearby, so much the better. But not all raccoons are so lucky. Forests have been cleared in many places. Houses have replaced trees. So what can raccoons do? They move into open attics, basements, sewer drains, and garages. On farms, raccoons move into sheds and barns.

When a raccoon does find a den, it doesn't live there for very long. It may stay for a few days. Then it goes off to search for food. The raccoon may return to its home. But more likely, it will find another hideaway.

Raccoon in
a hollow tree

What Do Raccoons Do at Night?

Lots of things! Raccoons are mostly nocturnal *(nahk TUR nuhl)*, or active at night. Usually, they sleep during the day and then go out at night in search of food.

Most often, raccoons leave their dens soon after sunset. They head straight for the nearest food source. Ponds, rivers, and lakes supply their favorite meals. Farm fields offer corn and other vegetables. Garbage cans in areas where people live provide tasty surprises.

At sunrise, tired raccoons find dens to snuggle up in for a long day's rest. However, sometimes raccoons also hunt for food during the day.

Raccoons at night

Do Raccoons Hibernate in Winter?

Raccoons do not really hibernate. Animals that hibernate go into a deep sleep that can last for most of the winter. Their heart rates slow down, and their body temperatures drop.

While raccoons don't hibernate, those that live in cold climates sleep for long periods of time during winter. They may stay in their dens for several weeks at a time. But on mild days, these raccoons often wake up. They go out in search of food. Once the weather gets cold again, they return to their dens and go back to sleep.

During their long periods of sleep, raccoons do not eat. Without food, they can lose up to one-half of their total weight! To prepare for these difficult times, raccoons eat more than usual in late summer and fall. This adds more and more fat to their bodies. Raccoons rely on this fat to survive cold winters.

Raccoons at rest

Are Raccoons Loners?

Most raccoons are loners. They spend a lot of time alone—especially if they are males.

A male raccoon lives in a den with a female only during mating season. The male leaves the den long before the baby raccoons are born.

Of course, a mother raccoon must stay with her babies, or cubs. As mammals, the cubs need to be nursed. Cubs usually stay with their mother until the end of their first winter. After they leave, she will be alone until she mates and gives birth to a new family.

During a harsh winter, a group of raccoons may band together. This group can consist of many females, but only one male. The group may share a den during the winter. But once spring arrives, most go their separate ways.

Lone raccoon

How Does a Mother Raccoon Care for Her Cubs?

A female raccoon can give birth to up to eight babies at once, usually in the spring. Before the babies are born, the expectant mother looks for a den high off the ground where she will give birth. An elevated den helps protect the cubs from many kinds of enemies.

Newborn cubs are both blind and deaf. They weigh about 2 1/2 ounces (71 grams) and are about 6 1/2 inches (16.5 centimeters) long. Their tails make up about one-third of their length!

The small and helpless cubs depend on their mother for food and protection. A mother raccoon cares for her cubs by nursing them with her milk. Her milk helps the cubs grow stronger. A mother raccoon also cares for her young just by lying with them. As the cubs snuggle up to her, her body gives off heat that helps keep them warm.

28

Mother raccoon
with cubs

How Do Cubs Become Adults?

By the time the cubs are 5 to 9 weeks old, they are ready to explore areas outside their den. So the mother then moves them to a den closer to the ground. When they are about 8 to 11 weeks old, she takes them with her to search for food. By 16 weeks, the cubs are weaned off their mother's milk. From this point on, the cubs must find their own food.

Most raccoon cubs spend their first winter sharing a den with their mother. But by spring, all offspring set off on their own.

The first order of business for the young raccoons is to find their own territory. By the end of their first year, they will be able to mate and have cubs. In the wild, raccoons can live to be about 5 years old.

Raccoon cubs

Do Raccoons Travel Much?

Yes, they do. How far raccoons travel depends on several things. They move around looking for food, water, and dens. If these things are close by, raccoons don't need to roam very far.

Both male and female raccoons form territories. A male raccoon does this by rubbing against a tree or a rock. Doing this leaves a scent that warns other males to stay away.

A male raccoon usually keeps a territory to himself, but sometimes females may share part of it with him. A male's territory covers about 100 to 250 acres (40 to 100 hectares). However, a male may roam as far as 10 miles (16 kilometers) to get food or to find a mate.

A female raccoon usually has a much smaller territory. Since she is often caring for a family, she is less able to travel. A mother raccoon must stay put in one den until her young are ready to explore outside the den.

Raccoon on the move

33

Who Are Enemies of Raccoons?

Like most animals living in the wild, raccoons have many enemies. Their enemies include cougars, jaguars, coyotes, foxes, and some kinds of owls. But their worst enemies of all are humans and dogs.

Adult raccoons can be ferocious when they are cornered. They have sharp teeth, which they use to defend themselves. They are quite capable of putting up a good fight. And their thick fur helps protect them against bites and other types of attacks.

Raccoons are quick runners, but they are not always fast enough to flee from large enemies. But with their sharp claws, raccoons are good tree climbers. If they see or smell an enemy, they can escape by scampering up a tree.

Raccoon fleeing
from coyote

Do Crab-Eating Raccoons Eat Only Crabs?

No, but crabs are a favorite food of crab-eating raccoons. Besides crabs, these raccoons eat crayfish, frogs, and other freshwater animals. But, like their northern cousins, they'll eat just about anything if they get hungry enough.

Although crab-eating raccoons and northern raccoons are a lot alike, there are differences between them. Crab-eating raccoons are semiaquatic *(SEHM ee uh KWAT ihk)*. This means that they spend much of their time in the water. Crab-eating raccoons also have thinner fur. This makes them appear more slender. And their tails are less bushy.

Crab-eating raccoons have stronger claws than northern raccoons do. They also have stronger molars, or teeth used for grinding. This may be nature's way of helping crab-eating raccoons crack the crabs and other shellfish they love to eat.

Crab-eating raccoons

Are Ringtails Raccoons, Too?

Ringtails are not raccoons, but they are close relatives. Like raccoons, they have long, bushy tails. But ringtails have more rings on their tails than most raccoons do. Ringtails usually have 16 to 18 black-and-white rings on their tails!

Ringtails also have rings around their eyes. Their eyes are large and dark. They are outlined by black hairs that are, in turn, surrounded by large white rings of hair.

Ringtails live mostly on rocky plateaus that have at least a few trees and a source of water. These animals are very excellent climbers. They can climb up canyon walls and over rocky ledges. They can even climb up narrow crevices in rock formations. How can ringtails do this? They put all their feet on one wall and press their backs against the other wall!

Ringtail

How Is a Ringtail Like a Cat?

A ringtail is about the same size as a housecat. It walks like a cat, too. While it may look as if a cat's whole foot touches the ground when it's walking, the cat is really walking only on its toes. The ringtail walks on its toes, too. The ringtail is the only raccoon relative that walks this way. The North American ringtail also has claws that can be drawn partly back into its paws—just as a cat's claws can be.

The grooming habits of a ringtail are also like those of a cat. Both animals lick their front paws. Then they use their damp paws to clean their ears, cheeks, and noses.

When it's angry, a ringtail acts like a cat, too. It hisses and raises the fur on its tail, just as a cat does. A ringtail has so much in common with a cat, it's easy to see why it's sometimes called a ringtail cat.

Ringtail

Just What Is a Cacomistle?

A cacomistle is a close relative of the ringtail. But instead of living in rocky areas as the ringtail does, the cacomistle lives in dense, moist forests. The cacomistle is arboreal *(ahr BAWR ee uhl)*. That means that it spends much of its time living up in trees.

Both the ringtail and cacomistle have long, thin bodies with long, bushy tails. But there are ways to tell these two raccoon relatives apart. For example, a cacomistle doesn't walk on its toes as a ringtail does. Rather, a cacomistle walks on the soles of its feet as other raccoon family members do. Usually, a cacomistle is slightly larger than a ringtail, too.

Cacomistle

What Is a Coati's Nose Good For?

The coati is a raccoon relative with a very long nose. Its nose is good for searching through leaves, crevices, and holes to find its favorite foods. These include insects, fruits, snails, mice, lizards, and bird eggs.

A coati also has a long tail—just as other raccoon relatives do. But a coati's tail is longer than its head *and* its body together! A coati spends much of its time with its tail held straight up high. This helps a coati keep its balance, especially when climbing and when leaping from branch to branch.

White-nosed coati

Do Coatis Like Company?

Female coatis like company. They often live in large groups, or bands, that have 20 to 40 members.

Group living has many advantages. Mother coatis help care for each other's young. The group also looks for food together. With so many coatis, they can spread out across a large area and find more food. And with so many pairs of eyes, they can also spot enemies before they attack. Adult female coatis often join together to frighten off their enemies.

A male coati stays with a band only during mating season. Afterward, the females chase him away. This is to keep a male from eating a baby coati if he gets really hungry. Young male coatis can stay in the band until they are about 2 years old. Then the rest of the group chases the young males off, too.

Grooming is important to coatis. The females often groom each other and their young. They use their teeth, feet, and hands to comb each other's fur.

Band of coatis

Is the Kinkajou a Kind of Monkey?

No, the kinkajou is often mistaken for a monkey, but it is actually a raccoon relative. Like many species of monkeys, the kinkajou lives in trees. Also, a kinkajou has a prehensile *(pree HEHN suhl)*, or grasping, tail as do many species of New World monkeys.

The kinkajou is the only raccoon family member with a prehensile tail. It makes traveling among the trees easy. When a kinkajou moves from branch to branch, its tail keeps a solid grip on one branch until its feet find good support on the next.

A kinkajou's tail also helps it get its favorite food— fruit. When a kinkajou sees a tasty fruit dangling below, the animal wraps its tail around a branch. Then it uses its hind legs for support and lowers its body upside down. With its hands free, the kinkajou can pick the fruit.

Kinkajou

How Else Does a Kinkajou Use Its Tail?

A mother kinkajou uses her tail to care for her baby. The kinkajou usually gives birth to just one baby at a time. This way, a mother kinkajou can give her baby plenty of attention. One way a mother kinkajou cares for her baby is by cuddling it. But she doesn't use her hands to do this—she cuddles it with her tail!

When a baby kinkajou is frightened, it hisses. The mother makes a soft chirping sound to calm the offspring. But if there really is danger nearby, the mother will carry her baby to safety by grabbing it in her mouth by its scruff, or the back of its neck. This is the way a cat carries its kittens.

A mother kinkajou nurses her baby for its first seven weeks. After that, the baby begins to eat some solid foods in addition to nursing. By 4 months, a young kinkajou, like the one pictured here, can find its own food.

Young kinkajou

Which Raccoon Relative Is a Real Stinker?

That's easy—the olingo *(AHL ihn goh)* is a stinker! The olingo may seem like a skunk in this respect, but it is a raccoon relative. In fact, the olingo looks a lot like a kinkajou. Both animals live in trees in tropical rain forests, too. They are even sometimes found living near one another. The easiest way to tell them apart is by their scents.

The olingo has a good reason to stink. It uses its smell to scare off its enemies. An olingo has a pair of scent glands near the base of its tail. When frightened or attacked, the olingo empties these glands. This releases a smell that is usually strong enough to make an enemy run away from the olingo as fast as it can!

The olingo has other good ways to protect itself, too. It can growl loudly, make shrill calls, and sound off with shrieking alarm sounds. It is also an excellent climber and jumper. It can quickly travel through tree branches to escape an attack.

Olingo

Where Do Red Pandas Fit In?

Most scientists group red pandas with the raccoon family because these animals and raccoons have much in common. Like other raccoon relatives, red pandas have long, bushy tails and markings on the fur of their faces. And, like raccoons, they can hold objects with their front paws.

Red pandas may be raccoon relatives, but they live far away from the rest of this animal family! All other raccoon relatives live in North, Central, and South America, but red pandas live in Asia. They make their homes in bamboo forests high in the Himalaya *(HIHM uh LAY uh)*. There, they can find plenty of their favorite food—bamboo leaves.

Red pandas are also similar to giant pandas. Like red pandas, giant pandas live in Asia and eat bamboo. At one time, giant pandas were considered members of the raccoon family. Most scientists now classify giant pandas with bears. But some scientists believe red pandas and giant pandas should be classified together in their own group.

Red panda

Does a Red Panda Have Thumbs?

A red panda does have thumbs. In fact, it has two thumbs on each forepaw! One thumb is a true thumb that is actually used like a finger. The other thumb is really a special bone on the wrist of each forepaw. This "false" thumb helps in climbing and grasping bamboo. This unusual bone is also found on the giant panda.

Bamboo is the red panda's food of choice. The animal uses the extra thumb on each paw to hold onto the bamboo stems. The red panda enjoys other foods, too. It also feeds on fruits, berries, roots, lichens, insects, bird eggs, and small rodents.

The red panda is a good climber. It spends most of its day sleeping and resting on the branches of trees. It usually comes to the ground to search for food at dawn and dusk.

Red panda

Do These Relatives Look a Lot Alike?

As you can see from this chart, raccoon relatives do look a lot alike. They are close in size and shape. Many have interesting markings on their faces. And, of course, they all have beautiful tails!

But just like any family, each member of this animal family stands out in its own way. Raccoons are known for their black masks and arched backs. The coati's long nose is its special feature. The cacomistle has faint rings on its tail compared to the dark rings of its closest relative, the ringtail. The kinkajou is the only member of this family whose tail has no rings. The olingo looks as if it could be the kinkajou's twin, except its tail has rings. And the red panda has ears outlined in white, a dark red coat, and the bushiest tail of all.

58

Northern raccoon

Ringtail

Crab-eating raccoon

Kinkajou

Olingo

Coati

Cacomistle

Red panda

Are These Animals in Danger?

Many of these animals are in danger because they are losing their habitats. Cacomistles, olingos, and kinkajous all live in trees in forests. Red pandas depend on bamboo forests for their diet. If people continue to cut down these forests, these raccoon relatives will soon have nowhere left to live.

There is good news, though, for the red panda. The Chinese government has established preserves of bamboo-rich land to protect the red panda's food source. More efforts like this are needed to ensure that the red panda and other raccoon relatives will be here for a long time to come.

While some raccoon relatives are in danger, others are thriving. Northern raccoons and other raccoons adapt well to their surroundings. These animals can live almost anywhere. Because of this, they continue to have a large population.

Kinkajou

Raccoon Relative Fun Facts

→ The name *raccoon* comes from the Native American Algonquin language and means "he scratches with his hands."

→ Ringtails were once called "miners' cats." They were kept in mines to kill rodents.

→ Coatis are also known as hog-nosed coons because of their long snouts.

→ Red pandas are also known as wahs, lesser pandas, Himalayan raccoons, and red cat bears.

→ In cold weather, ringtails may wrap their tails around their bodies to stay warm.

→ Another name for a kinkajou is a "honey bear." This raccoon relative extends its long, thin tongue to extract honey from beehives.

Glossary

arboreal Living in or among trees.

bamboo A woody or treelike grass with a tall, hollow stem.

band A large group of female coatis.

canine A large, pointed tooth.

canyon A narrow valley with high, steep sides.

carnivore An animal that eats meat.

crevice A narrow crack or a split.

cub A baby raccoon.

den A home of some land animals.

forepaw A front paw.

grizzled Streaked with gray.

hibernate To sleep through the cold months.

mammal A warm-blooded animal that feeds its young on the mother's milk.

molar A broad tooth with a flat surface used for grinding.

nocturnal Active at night.

plateau A large plain or flat area.

prehensile Capable of grasping and holding by wrapping around.

preserve A place where wild animals are kept and protected.

procyonids An animal family that includes raccoons and their relatives.

scavenger An animal that feeds on food left by other animals and humans.

semiaquatic Living close to water or spending time in water.

territory An area of land that an animal keeps for itself.

wean To get a young animal used to food other than its mother's milk.

Index

(**Boldface** indicates a photo, map, or illustration.)

For more information about raccoons and their relatives, try these resources:

Clever Raccoons, by Kristen L. Nelson, Lerner Publications Company, 2000.

Raccoon, by Allan Fowler, Children's Press. 2000.

Raccoons for Kids: Ringed Tails and Wild Ideas, by Jeff Fair, NorthWord Press, Inc., 1994.

http://www.nhptv.org/natureworks/raccoon.htm

http://www.pbs.org/edens/bhutan/a_rp.htm

http://www.thebigzoo.com/Animals/Raccoon.asp

Procyonid Classification

Scientists classify animals by placing them into groups. The animal kingdom is a group that contains all the world's animals. Phylum, class, order, and family are smaller groups. Each phylum contains many classes. A class contains orders, an order contains families, and a family contains individual species. Each species also has its own scientific name. Here is how the animals in this book fit in to this system.

Animals with backbones and their relatives (Phylum Chordata)
Mammals (Class Mammalia)
Carnivores (Order Carnivora)
Racoons and their relatives (Family Procyonidae)

Cacomistle . . . . *Bassariscus sumichrasti*

Crab-eating raccoon . . . . *Procyon cancrivorus*

Kinkajou . . . . *Potos flavus*

Northern raccoon . . . . *Procyon lotor*

Olingo . . . . *Bassaricyon gabbii*

Red (lesser) panda . . . . *Ailurus fulgens*

Ringtail . . . . *Bassariscus astutus*

White-nosed coati . . . . *Nasua narica*

The
Complete Guide to
FRAMING

Techniques ◆ *Materials*

The
Complete Guide to
FRAMING

Techniques ◆ *Materials*

JENNY RODWELL & GEORGE SHORT

North
Light

A QUARTO BOOK

Copyright © 1986 Quarto Publishing Ltd

Published in North America by
North Light, an imprint of Writer's Digest Books
9933 Alliance Road
Cincinnati, Ohio 45242

ISBN 0-89134-129-3

This book was designed and produced by
Quarto Publishing Ltd
The Old Brewery, 6 Blundell Street
London N7 9BH

Senior editor Jane Laing

Art editor Moira Clinch

Editorial Polly Powell, Michelle Newton

Designer Rita Wuthrich
Design assistants Anthony Bussey, Fraser
Newman, Ursula Dawson

Illustrators Ray Brown, Fraser Newman, Mick Hill
Photographers Mac Campeanu, John Heseltine

Consultants Mike Crossman, Peter Worley and
staff at the Newgate Gallery, London, Christine
Ovel, Aidan Walker
Indexer Richard Bird

Art director Nigel Osborne
Editorial director Jim Miles

Typeset by Facsimile Graphics Ltd, Coggeshall
Paste-up by Elly King, Dave Evans
Colour origination by Rainbow Graphic Arts Co
Ltd, Hong Kong
Printed by Lee Fung Asco Printers Ltd, Hong Kong

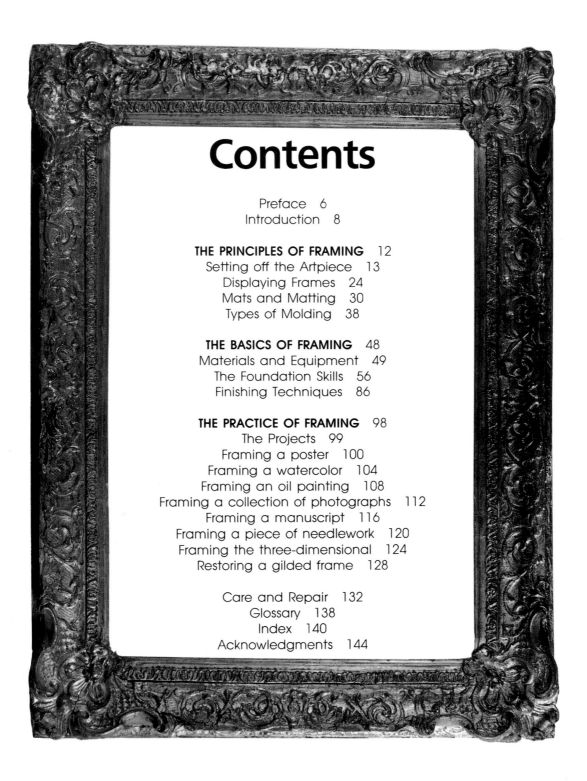

Contents

Preface

Whether a gilded border of ornate decorations or a simple band of metal, the frame plays a major role in the total visual impact of an artpiece, enhancing or seriously distorting the overall effect of the image. The most suitable choice is not always the most obvious one and this book offers valuable guidelines on selecting frames for a wide variety of artpieces, including the three-dimensional. In many cases you will be unable to find a perfectly suitable ready-made frame and will want to make your own. The *Complete Guide to Framing* tells you how.

The basic principles and techniques of framing and matting are clearly explained and step-by-step illustrated instructions guide you through all the foundation skills of picture framing, from measuring the artpiece to giving your frames a special finish. A large project section, covering a wide range of framing techniques, will enable you to complete different types of frame for different types of artwork. There is a section on the tools and materials needed — it always pays to buy the best you can afford; cheap tools can let you down badly — and a section on the care and repair of both frames and artworks, which will prove especially useful to all those interested in buying second-hand frames and tailoring them to their own requirements. Many damaged frames can be successfully renovated and even the oldest picture frames can usually be stripped of plaster and gilt and the wooden base used as the foundation for one of your own finishes.

Introduction

from an artpiece into the surrounding room. A block of color in a picture will "jump out" if there is a similar color nearby and the picture is not framed. The frame defines the extent of the artpiece and stops this subconscious action of the human eye. It plays exactly the same role in preventing the surface of a picture from becoming merged and confused with the surrounding surface, such as a patterned wallpaper or a textured wall surface.

On a more practical level, the frame protects the artwork from damage. It guards against general wear and tear and against accident when an artwork is being handled.

THE DEVELOPMENT OF FRAMING

In the ancient classical world, frames were made mainly for mirrors. The Romans and Greeks painted frescos directly onto walls without frames as they are now known. Meanwhile, the Oriental civilizations were developing their own distinct attitude toward paintings. Chinese and Japanese artists painted their works upon folding screens, which divided rooms, and scrolls, which were hung directly on the wall without frames.

In Medieval times, artists began painting onto the slightly hollowed surface of wooden panels and the raised edges, often decorated with separate motifs, gradually developed into a formal picture frame. To begin with frames were frequently part of the solid piece, rather than existing in their own right, and the first separate frames were imitations of their original architectural surroundings — an environment which

A lthough there have been some spectacular exceptions, such as the ancient cave paintings and some murals, a frame is normally needed to act as a boundary. It therefore plays an important role in the composition of a picture. A church steeple in a landscape painting, for instance, will often be slightly offset, rather than centered, to give a more interesting composition but this is effective only if the limits to the picture are obvious. For, without limits, the whole idea of a composition becomes meaningless and the shapes in the picture merge into the surroundings.

The frame also prevents the "escape" of colors

The emerging frame
*Rich bands of intricate
decoration surround these
paintings of the early
Renaissance. The setting,
like the picture itself, was
inspired by religion and
given up to the glory of
God. Intricate patterns
(left)* are worked around
the *Lamentation over the
Body of Christ by Giotto.
The triptych* Madonna
and Child *by Duccio
(above) is an altarpiece
painted into hinged,
recessed panels which are
the forerunners of the
modern frame.*

Imitating architecture
*Attempts to imitate
architectural designs led
to the creation of styles
which gradually evolved
into the modern frame.
On each side of the
Baptism by della
Francesca (left) stand two
pilasters, fake 'pillars,'
such as would be found
on a doorway or
impressive window recess.*

The simple, sombre frame surrounding Blake's watercolor on wood, The Body of Abel Found by Adam and Eve *(above), highlights the dramatic nature of the painting.*

The contemporary artist, Howard Hodgkin, has incorporated the frame into his oil painting on wood, D H in Hollywood *(right) to vivid and complementary effect.*

was ornate and ecclesiastical. As cathedrals and larger churches were built they demanded even grander architecture. The frame, like the architecture, became more elaborate, as can be seen in the lavish arches, pinnacles and carvings around the Polyptych altarpiece in the Strozzi Chapel, Santa Maria Novella, Florence, by Andrea Orcagna (*c.* 1308–1368). One style which became popular was the Tabernacle frame, a literal imitation of a window recess in which pilasters, make-believe 'pillars' or flattened versions of columns, flanked the painting. The *Madonna and Child with Saints and Donors* in Santo Spirito, Florence, by Filippino Lippi (c. 1457–1504), provides an outstanding example of such a Tabernacle frame.

The real breakthrough for the picture frame came in the late fifteenth and early sixteenth centuries when painters began to see themselves as artists in their own right and not simply as servants of architects. They required frames to set their paintings apart from their surroundings. Some of the best frames ever made date from this period. One of the new styles to evolve was the Tondo or circular type exemplified by the intricately carved, wide, gilded frame surrounding the *Holy Family* by Michelangelo, to be found in the Uffizi Gallery in Florence.

Sixteenth-century frame makers began moving toward a more restrained style and the frame grad-

ually became more harmonious with the picture within. Soon, the wealthier classes began seeking paintings for their own homes. Art was no longer merely for public display and it became a product which increasingly needed to be transported after being bought by an individual; and so picture frames became a practical necessity.

As painters became more in demand, they found they had little time to make their own frames. They passed the work on to their apprentices and to outside specialists and so frame making became a skilled craft with its own separate place in the art industry. Increasingly the frame became the property of the cabinet maker and it changed in style as the style of furniture changed. Materials became more sophisticated; in Puritan-influenced northern Europe exotic woods replaced gaudy gilded moldings.

From time to time conflicts arose between the painter and the frame maker. In the sixteenth century, for instance, frame makers tried to outdo each other and the frames often outshone the paintings, placing them in settings which were extremely elaborate and often inlaid with materials such as jewels, mother of pearl and ivory. The rich rococo style of architecture and interior decoration, popular in early eighteenth-century France, was reflected in frames, and, although a simpler fashion was introduced with the neoclassical revival in Europe in the late part of that century, the rococo designs kept returning. One of these styles, popular for many years, was the Lawrence frame, named after Sir Thomas Lawrence (1769–1830), a fashionable British portrait painter.

With the growth of Modernism in the early twentieth century, frames were widely denounced as over-elaborate and unnecessary visual competition for the picture. Artists increasingly chose simple frames. Some disregarded the traditional restrictions of the frame, such as the American abstract expressionist, Jackson Pollock (1912–1956), who painted huge canvases of dripping and spattered colors, creating an overall image and generating an energy which many argued would have been inappropriate if contained in a fixed wall-piece. Supporters of this idea talked of a 'visual splash' of color and shape, which, they argued, did not fit into the conventions of pictorial composition and therefore did not require a frame. During the same period, some museums removed more ornate frames from recent paintings and replaced them with simple ones.

In more recent years, however, there has been a definite revival of interest in, and respect for, the frame. There has also been a rise in the popularity of elaborate frames. Critics report that a number of artists have turned to the frame for its ability to enhance and even interact with the painted surface. Several contemporary artists have fitted frames specially designed to interact with their pictures. For example, two modern American painters, the abstract artist Marsden Hartley and the figurative painter Maurice Prendergast, sometimes make their own frames to accord with their images and Georgia O'Keefe, another American artist, has solid metal frames specially made to complement her work.

Altering or abandoning the frame is not a new idea. During the Baroque period, which began in Europe in the early seventeenth century, many paintings were reframed in a more ornate style. The gold leaf of some of the new frames introduced to the Pitti Palace in Florence, for instance, was so bright that some said it distracted seriously from the paintings. In the early nineteenth century, Napoleon had many paintings in the Louvre reframed in the then fashionable Empire style.

The picture frame has endured throughout all these changes in fashion and looks set to continue indefinitely as the necessary boundary for most works of art. It has also increasingly come into its own among browsers of stalls and antique stores who wish to frame collections of old prints, maps, posters and other memorabilia.

The Principles of Framing

Setting off the Artpiece
◾
Displaying Frames
◾
Mats and Matting
◾
Types of Molding

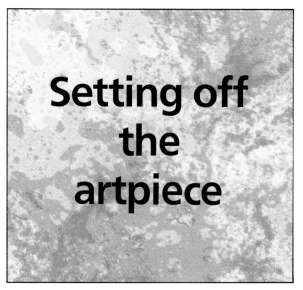

Setting off the artpiece

T here is really no such thing as the "right" frame for an artpiece — one correct frame which must belong to a particular image. A vast choice is open to the collector or framer and in the end the choice of frame is a matter of personal taste, which is why this is such a fascinating subject, appealing to the individualist.

There are some principles, however, which can be followed to advantage. They fall into two basic categories: the general and the specific. Different types of frames should be used for different types of artwork — oils, watercolors, posters, photographs and so on; and a frame should be chosen that enhances the individual characteristics of a particular artwork. In all cases, the artwork should dictate the frame and not vice versa. The style and color of the frame and mat should not fight the artwork for attention, nor should they detract from the image. Rather they should complement the image, drawing attention to it. If the viewer notices the frame or mat rather than the artwork, then they have failed.

There is a further interesting demarcation between old and new frames. An old frame is not necessarily the best choice for an old artpiece, nor a new frame for a new one. It is a question of style. You may decide that a new artpiece needs an antique-looking frame and, conversely, many old artworks, especially old photographs, look attractive in modern frames. Within these categories there is much scope for imagination. For instance, if you decide on an old-style frame, you are not confined to a genuinely antique one. There are many modern reproduction frames, and reproduction moldings can be bought and used to make your own "antiqued" version.

A host of ready-made new frames can also be purchased. The drawback here is the range of sizes available. Pictures, old prints, maps and any other items you may wish to frame do not fall easily into rigid categories of size and shape. You need spe-

cific proportions and this should be dictated by the artpiece rather than by the size of frame that happens to be available in a store.

For some projects, ready-made equipment — such as clip frames or other simple acrylic framing kits — can be useful. Generally speaking, though, you may find this too limiting as your interest grows. Kits for self-assembly frames are available in plastic, metal or wood but, again, the problem is the severely limited range of sizes and the fact that kits are usually available only in the plainest of styles.

One alternative to buying new frames is to turn to the bargain or junk market. Here you may find a greater range of sizes and styles, often at reasonable prices, because they are frequently damaged.

No matter what kind of frame you decide on, one factor becomes increasingly important as you gain in expertise. This is the need to match the frame to the subject being framed. This section takes a look at the wide variety of artpieces you might wish to frame and offers general guidelines on the most suitable kinds of frames, mats and finishes. For a more detailed discussion on mats and matting, and moldings see pages 30–37 and 38–47. Details on specific picture-framing techniques are given on pages 56–85.

OILS AND ACRYLICS
Pictures in oils or acrylics are usually painted onto canvas stretchers (the canvas stretched taut over a framework of wooden slats), canvas-covered boards, or hardboard. With the stretcher, a traditional surface for oils, extra care has to be taken when framing because the painting is often slightly asymmetrical, the thickness of the canvas varies round the edge, and the slats can cause problems.

As a general rule, paintings in oils or acrylics are not glazed — that is, they are not covered by glass — although sometimes glass is used to provide protection, especially with smaller paintings, when it may also actively enhance the picture.

Oil and acrylic paintings usually have a vigorous presence. There are exceptions but, broadly speaking, the very nature of oil and acrylic paints gives a texture that makes the painting stand out more boldly than would a watercolor or print, especially when the artist has used them in a thick or impastoed manner. When framing most oil paintings, therefore, you are dealing with something which is in relief, literally "standing out from the wall."

It is this that governs your choice of frame; it also helps to broaden the choice. You can sometimes make do with narrow frames, such as wooden or metal strips, that do not cover any of the surface of the painting but are merely tacked onto the edge of the stretcher. This is a suitable approach if the painting is strong enough to stand out on its own and a slim boundary will suffice.

On the other hand, a strong painting can also take a strong frame. This is especially useful in the

Oil and acrylic
The framers' molding around this picture (above) gives a strong surround to this rather subdued picture, without overpowering it. The green mat surrounding the rural scene (above right) picks out the greens in the picture. The *polished wooden frame gives it a solid and permanent look. The garden scene (right) is thickly painted with bold colors, using a lot of greens, and the renovated wooden frame complements these textures and colors.*

case of a small painting. The presence here of a wider frame will help to focus the eye onto the painting itself, which, although small in size, will still be bold enough not to be dominated by the frame. With larger paintings, the freedom of choice is total. They can stand up to 'rougher' stylistic treatment.

WATERCOLORS

Unlike oils and acrylics, watercolors can suffer terribly from their frames. Generally, watercolors have delicate, washy surfaces and all too often one sees a thinly painted watercolor languishing inside an intricate or heavy frame that makes the picture look as if it is fading away.

By tradition, watercolor frames have been rather unadventurous. They tend to have a subdued look, reflecting the muted tones of the picture they contain. The rugged moorlands or soft trees mellowly depicted by a typical watercolorist like John Sell Cotman (1782–1842) hang on many walls inside frames which are necessarily low key, with a yellowing, dusty look. This quiet framing style is suited to older watercolors — unfortunately, it has become a tradition for *all* types of watercolors. Some modern pictures, however, deserve a brighter context; the concentrated, luminous colors which many modern watercolorists use can stand up to a more vibrant frame.

Nearly all watercolors stand behind a 'mat,' a cardboard 'frame' within the actual frame. This creates a broad expanse of space, providing a sympathetic surround that separates the image from the hard edge of the frame. Since watercolor paints are transparent, they give a fragile, ethereal image and it is generally not a good idea to surround them with an opaque or densely colored mat. This

Watercolors
A soft watercolor of Durham Town is given a sympathetic dark brown mat in a gold, antiqued frame (above). The beveled edge of the mat is lined with antique gold to match the gold on the frame. A large frame with a simple molding surrounds a cream mat for this small watercolor (left).

explains why traditional watercolor mats are white, cream or pastel-colored. Again, there are exceptions but these are best done consciously — if you use a bright or dark mat, choose it for a specific reason.

Glass is nearly always used to cover watercolor pictures, as they are far less durable than oils or acrylics. Dust is a great enemy of watercolors, making them dull and dark. Moisture wrinkles the paper and, in extreme conditions, causes the spots of brown mildew known as 'foxing,' which can be seen on many older prints and watercolors.

Although the mat is often a broad border around the picture — and the smaller the picture, the bigger the mat can be in contrast — the frame itself should be narrow. Visually, it should make as little fuss as possible, so as not to detract from the picture.

A common characteristic of watercolors is that the paint is rarely taken right up to the edge of the paper. This gives the framer the choice of leaving this unpainted area showing or cropping it closely. Usually, watercolors are best left with the 'random edge' uncropped because this enables the viewer to see how the washes of paint are affected by the paper and the picture benefits from the irregular expanse around its composition.

PASTELS

Pastel paintings, like watercolors, are usually framed by a mat and a frame, and the advice given for matting and framing watercolors *(see page 14)* applies equally well to pastels.

Pastels are fine chalks and smudge easily. Therefore, in addition to fixing the painting with a fixative spray, a double mat is often used to keep the pastel away from the glass.

PHOTOGRAPHS

Old sepia photographs, popular with collectors, can be greatly enhanced by being framed in traditional style, in keeping with their nostaligic appearance. However, you can use a modern mat and frame to good effect with some images.

With modern photographs, you can rarely afford to take such liberties. Most modern photographs belong firmly to their own era and usually demand a modern frame.

Some framers like to trim off the white edges round photographs but this is not advisable when dealing with the older ones, as the edges often contain fascinating signatures, or captions scribbled in faded ink, or fancy edging reflecting bygone fashions. These characteristics deserve to be preserved and they can be included in the visual whole of the frame. Treatment similar to that of a watercolor is best here: use a neutral-colored mat and leave the captioned edge of the photograph visible inside. Neutral colors for mats work well with modern photographs, although sometimes a contemporary black-and-white photograph can be set off by a more brightly colored mat.

With an old portrait photograph, there is plenty of scope. Again, it would probably be unsuitable to crop it and give it a modern setting. A fabric mat, damask or lace perhaps, gives a period touch to a photograph. Alternatively, you could use old-fashioned marbled paper or vellum. In some cases, if the photograph is in good condition, it is possible to frame it directly, without using a mat. This may be especially effective in cases where older photographs have been 'vignetted' — that is, where the image is isolated in the center of a slightly faded and misty-looking background.

One remarkable way to give a sympathetic setting to most old photographs is to use a fabric-covered frame. Leather can be glued onto a wooden frame, adding textural interest to the picture as a whole. Brown or olive green leather, for instance, works well with the warm tones of old

The collection of photographs (above, far left) is given cohesion by the formal arrangement and each one is made much more distinctive by the ruled lines that surround each photograph (see project, page 112). The sepia photograph (below, far left) is given a touch of color by the fine strips of green and mid-brown inlay set in the wooden frame. The double mat beautifully sets off the modern print (left). By inserting strips of black into the light-colored frame (above), the eye is drawn to the simple black-and-white print.

sepia photographs but any thick material can be used, including velvet and suede.

You can be much more boisterous in the treatment of modern photographs: black-and-white prints can be contrasted with brightly colored surrounds; colored photographs can be placed in a black-and-white setting or in a setting or color which repeats a theme present in the photograph.

Modern photographs usually look their best in an austere setting, although this depends on the subject. A picture in the style of a contemporary photographer such as Ansell Adams, for instance, with its stark quality, sharply defined shapes and contrasting tones would be shown to best advantage in a simple frame — perhaps just a narrow metallic band or a plain black frame. Most modern photographs look best with as little distraction as possible and simple acrylic clipboards are usually sufficient, especially if the picture is to be hung against a plain background.

In modern photo-journalism the image is all-important and the subject is sometimes a serious one, often making a social comment or recording some dramatic event. Again, a fussy frame would be distracting and inappropriate.

PRINTS
There is a brisk market nowadays for prints of all kinds and ages, from faded illustrations torn from old books to bright, graphic lithographs produced by modern artists. As with photographs, contemporary prints can be freely interpreted when it comes to choosing a frame. Simple frames, such as those made of colored plastic or metal strip, often look effective on strong modern designs.

There is one general rule which applies to both old and new prints: leave the edge of the print showing. In a good print, this edge should be a crisp line but all edges are interesting because they show how the plate is registered — that is, how the colors are laid on top of each other, so that they meet in the exact positions in the composition. With etch-

Posters
Because posters have such a strong graphic content, they nearly always require the simplest of frames. A blue mat and a flat blue frame surround the poster (above). In some cases, posters can look attractive without any surround at all—as with the poster (left), which has been clipped onto a backing board beneath glass. Transparent acrylic clips were used and the backing board was edged with plain wooden strips to give a neater edge (see project, page 100).

The traditional look
This piece of modern needlework was given a traditional appearance by surrounding it with a velvet-covered slip and a mahogany molding.

Antique piece
This sampler requires an old-looking surround. It is well worth hunting for the right old-style frame for such an attractive piece.

ings, for instance, an indentation can be seen in the paper where the metal plate was pressed onto the damp paper. By leaving this "key" intact when you frame the print, you display a facet of the production which many will find interesting.

Old prints can be given a new lease of life by reframing them. The white surround is often discolored and frequently there will be blotches of mold, or foxing, which is caused by a chemical reaction of moisture in the atmosphere with the iron content in the paper. By reframing the print and giving it a mat, you can often cover up such defects. You will also have had an opportunity to clean up the print before reframing it. Cleaning, care and maintenance is covered in Care and Repair.

When reframing, you do not necessarily have to use an exact replica of the original frame but it is best if you choose one that remains in character with the picture. For example, a modern steel frame would look wrong with an antique print. Experiment with one of the finishes discussed on pages 44–47: the frame could be enhanced perhaps by a gilding or by a patina — a softening tonal wash.

Old prints often have the title underneath the picture. Rather than obliterating this, it is better to cut a small window in the mat.

POSTERS

The inspiration for most posters came from the events for which they were produced to advertise. Thus they began as ephemeral things, pieces of art which were by nature temporary. It is therefore often inappropriate to give them a permanent-looking frame, as if they were classical artefacts. Posters, after all, were designed to stand alone, and they can look striking if this effect is preserved. A simple block mat or clip frame is enough. For details of this style of matting, see the poster project on pages 100–103.

Recently, posters have been more consciously aimed at being works of art in their own right and, there are many "art" posters on the market. Yet they still reflect the original bold styles and, like prints, look best when framed in a simple way.

NEEDLEWORK AND OTHER FABRIC IMAGES

The way to prevent a piece of treasured needlework, collage, weaving or silk-screen from becoming tattered or worn is to frame it. The piece of work should be stretched first around a board or similar surface, fixing it at the back with masking tape. Until this is done, it is impossible to know its correct measurements for framing.

Glass is needed to protect the piece but avoid placing glass directly onto the surface. An insert or some other means must be found to separate the fabric from the glass pane where the material could be distorted by pressure from the glass.

In the late nineteenth and early twentieth centuries in America and Europe, embroidered samplers were often placed in tortoiseshelled, woodgrained or otherwise decorated frames and you

Maps and documents The antique map of Africa (left) has been given a light wooden molding with green edges. Because there is a lot of space within the actual subject, it does not need a separate mat. A red mat with a traditional tiny black and gilt frame adds a theatrical formality to the small opera souvenir (below left). The simple black script on paper (below) is given a formal appearance by its plain red mat and polished wooden frame.

might like to preserve this traditon when framing or reframing such a piece; finishes are discussed on pages 44–47.

MAPS AND DOCUMENTS — OLD AND NEW

It is best to separate quite clearly in your mind the difference between framing a modern map or document and an antique one. The two types are found on the wall for entirely different reasons: the antique one is there mainly for its visual effect, a decorative piece of nostalgia or historic interest; the modern one is there as a colorful reference.

Maps

For the modern map, a simple clip frame or block mat is preferable — a businesslike frame. Some might feel that the style of the frame will make no difference and that a modern map could be set within an old-looking elaborate frame but you will probably find that the result will look incongruous.

Genuinely antique maps, or reproductions of antiques that convey the same atmosphere, are often seen in frames of polished wood such as maple and walnut — woods with warm colors. They can also look good in frames decorated with a special finish, such as imitation tortoiseshell or marble (see pages 93–97). Making a new frame for an old map provides an opportunity to carry out some finishing work to give the frame an antique look.

With an old map, the question immediately arises of whether to trim the edges to remove torn and grubby pieces of the paper edge. This is not advisable, especially if you have been lucky enough to get hold of a map which has not been interfered with too much over the years. Unfortunately, if the map is genuinely old, you are likely to find that it has

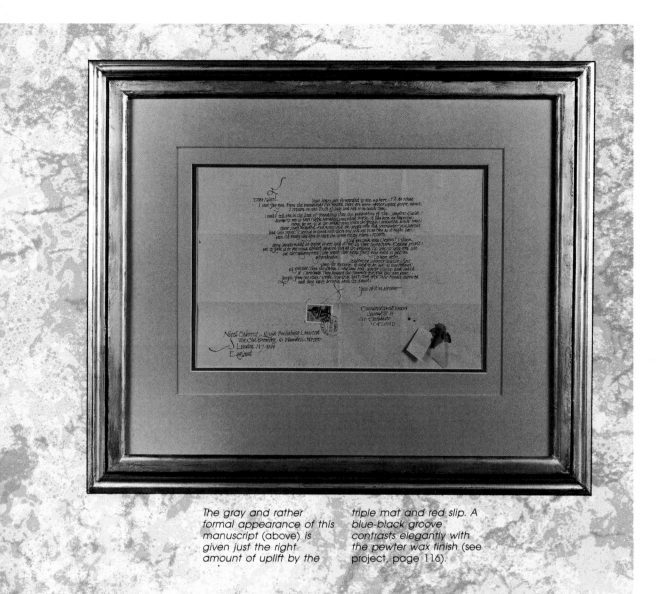

The gray and rather formal appearance of this manuscript (above) is given just the right amount of uplift by the triple mat and red slip. A blue-black groove contrasts elegantly with the pewter wax finish (see project, page 116).

already been trimmed too much, as different owners have forced it into available frames. Once removed, an edge cannot be replaced and the map will lose its value as well as the aesthetic effect of the original wide margin. Repair and cleaning of old maps and documents is explained on pages 136–137.

The broad margin which surrounds most old maps makes it generally undesirable to mat them. The margin itself, often with attractively aged and faded paper and interesting keys or titles, is a good enough 'mat' with which to surround the map.

With an old map, or any piece of archive document that you wish to preserve and frame, it is advisable to flatten out the original carefully and place it on a conservation board; the board should be specially purchased. Ordinary matting board will not do in this case as it absorbs the acid in the air,

and this will eventually soak through into the print and discolor or damage it.

Some interesting maps and documents, which you might wish to frame, are printed on both sides. In order that you can see both sides, a double-sided frame, usually a freestanding one, is necessary. Double-sided frames are often used when framing bonds and shares.

Documents

These also fit into two basic categories: the functional, such as a diploma, which is there to inform; and the decorative, such as a piece of calligraphy, an historic manuscript or an illuminated text. With the functional document, a simple frame is better: a plain narrow frame reflects its dignity. With the decorative piece, the choice is broader. A piece of writing is essentially flat, without the illusion of space

Pressed flowers
*The attraction of these pressed
flowers (above) lies partly in their
fragile and faded look. The
collector browsed through the junk
stores to find this fitting old, plain,
narrow frame.*

found in most pictures and, for this reason, it is often rewarding to give a spatial feeling to a piece of text by placing it in a frame with molding that projects outward to make the whole object three-dimensional. Illuminated lettering is often decorated with gold and bright colors. This can be pleasingly brought out by having gilt on the frame and perhaps adding a narrow strip of one of the colors contained in the text.

THE THREE-DIMENSIONAL

Many people like to display a three-dimensional set piece on the wall. This might be a collection of medals, or a collage made of shells, beads or other materials. Oriental fans, tiny pieces of carvings or sculpture, or arrangements of dried flowers can all look attractive on a wall.

This type of piece calls for a box-like frame, sometimes known as a display frame or 'shadow box,' so-called because when lit from an angle it can highlight the three-dimensional aspect of the piece

with shadows. The box is basically an ordinary frame but with a deeper insert.

Any subject which is likely to gather dust, such as dried flowers or a delicate fan, should be placed under glass. With the three-dimensional box, you can choose your own background to match the subject. If it is a Chinese fan, for instance, a piece of Chinese paper would make a good background; shells could be placed on a 'beach' effect made by gluing sand evenly across the back board. There is plenty of scope here for creativity.

Extra care is needed for work of a more enduring nature, such as ceramics, jewelry and small pieces of sculpture or antique glass. Such items stand out alone, and often need the simplest of settings. A piece of Roman glass, for instance, is intrinsically interesting and invites close inspection. Such a hard and glossy object would benefit from being placed on a simple, softly textured background which complements the centerpiece, such as coarse silk or linen.

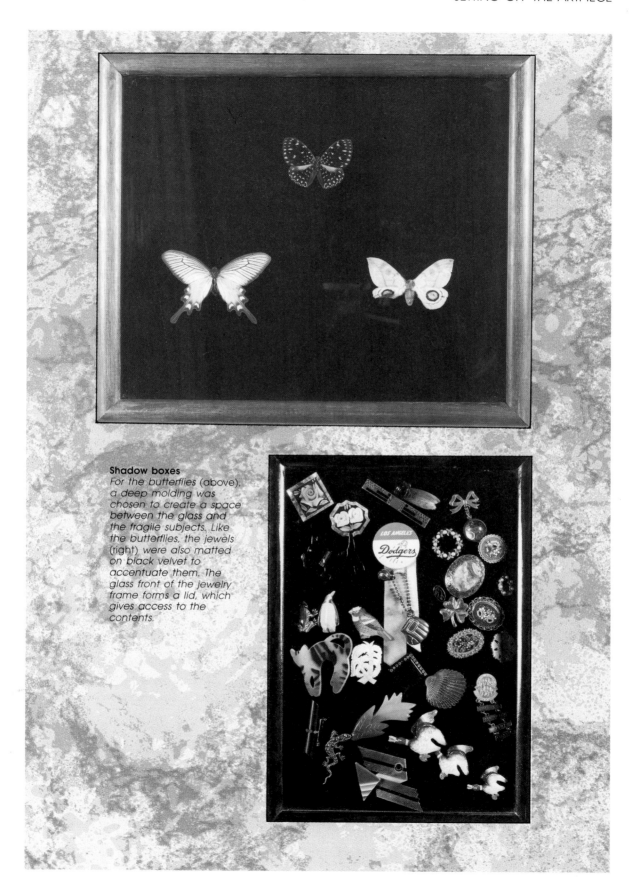

Shadow boxes
For the butterflies (above),
a deep molding was
chosen to create a space
between the glass and
the fragile subjects. Like
the butterflies, the jewels
(right) were also matted
on black velvet to
accentuate them. The
glass front of the jewelry
frame forms a lid, which
gives access to the
contents.

Displaying frames

There is a view — some might call it artistic snobbery — that it is wrong to consider how a painting will fit in with the decor of a room. Painting, they argue, is on a high aesthetic plane far superior to such mundane things as interior decorating. However, this argument ignores the fact that throughout its early history most art was created purely to complement its surroundings.

While the more experimental art forms play an undeniably important cultural role, it would be a pity if the pleasure of choosing pictures and frames to suit the home environment was lost and this section looks at the place of the frame within the larger environment of a room.

PLACING THE ARTPIECE

When deciding where to hang a framed artpiece, several practical points should be borne in mind. Heat can seriously damage the surface of paintings, especially oils, so avoid placing them directly above heaters. Not only will the rising heat damage the picture but dust and grease will also be carried upward and will gradually concentrate over the picture surface. If for some reason you cannot avoid placing a picture above a heater, then make sure that it is glazed. Artworks should also be kept free of damp and condensation. Direct sunlight can cause watercolors to fade; some pigments are especially vulnerable. A popular material used in modern watercolors is watercolor concentrate; some of these colors are particularly fugitive. Hang such paintings on walls that are not in the line of direct sunlight.

Aesthetic considerations are also important. If you have only one artpiece on a wall it is usually preferable to hang it so that the center of the artpiece aligns approximately with the average person's eye-level. This position will vary according to the room in which the artpiece is hung: if you wish to hang a set of pictures in a hallway, for instance, where people rarely sit, then eye-level should be

determined when standing; in a sitting-room, however, you should hang the pictures lower as people are likely to view them from a chair or sofa.

A small or narrow space — a hallway or corridor, for instance — is often ideal for small, detailed artpieces, where the interest lies in the content rather than in the general visual impact. A larger picture, however, where the viewer needs to stand back in order to take in the whole image, requires more space. It may look impressive at the end of a long corridor, or you could try placing it opposite the entrance to a room.

GROUPING AND ARRANGING

Often, the striking characteristic of a group of artpieces is their unity: they all seem to belong. This effect does not happen automatically; much thought is needed to achieve it. Attention should be given to the space between each artpiece. If the space is too narrow, the pictures will interfere with each other, whereas if there is too much space, the group will lose its cohesion.

Before hanging a group of pictures, it is a good idea to arrange them on the floor first, matching the shapes and colors. This will give you a reasonable

Vertical arrangement
The arrangement of the frames here (above) has an effect on the appearance of the interic of the hallways as a whole. The irregular

rectangles form a pillar of their own and complement the diagonal slope of the banisters and the curved arch of the open doorway.

Colorful abundance
Frames need not be regularly spaced in a formal way. They can often look attractive when thrown together at random, completely covering a wall to present an effect rather like an antique market or junk store. In the arrangement (right), a colorful mixture of antique and modern frames containing a variety of images creates an exciting impact.

The more formal approach
1 A few smaller frames can be ranged around a very large picture to good effect. Align the tops to give a formal cohesion to the group.
2 Four rectangular frames, each of a different size and proportion, can be given form by basing them on vertical and horizontal axes.
3 Arrange a variety of rectangular frames sitting on top and hanging underneath a hypothetical line.
4 This mixture of frames are arranged within what is in effect an overall 'frame'—the rectangle in which they are enclosed.
5 When arranging frames on the wall of a stairway, use imaginary verticals to provide form. In this way a 'scattered,' unrelated look is avoided.

Arranging and displaying
*Period frames are arranged
symmetrically and aligned with
a sideboard to give a neat
effect (top left). Circular objects
provide an interesting contrast
(center top). A set of framed
pictures (top right) gives a
formal appearance to this
elegant bedroom. A set of cards
is given form by the fan-shaped
frame (far left). As the frame is
transparent, its shape does not
disrupt the wall color. A
bathroom is enlivened with
framed documents and charts
(left). A dense arrangement of
pictures makes a feature of a
whole wall (right).*

representation of the final effect and the opportunity to experiment before you commit yourself.

One way of making a harmonious group from an array of different shapes and odd proportions is to line up either the tops or the bottoms of the pictures. If you are arranging a group of artpieces for an awkward space, such as the wall next to a staircase, it is not always practical to align them horizontally. In this case, the group spirit can be preserved by lining up the sides of the pictures so that there are regular 'columns' of space between them. Other groupings that can work well include square and circular formations. Experiment with different arrangements to see which suits your artworks best.

MIXING AND MATCHING FRAMES

A set of matching artpieces, or even very different ones, can be given unity by placing each one in an identical frame. This is especially effective if there are other things in the room which are visually 'busy,' such as patterned fabrics and wallpapers.

However, one of the most exciting forms of design for a group is to mix the frames, mixing not only the colors, shapes, styles and sizes but also old and new. Although a room that is decorated in a particular period style requires frames that do not jar with the style, most rooms are not designed in such a unified way. Rooms are more often designed according to personal taste and, over a period of years, result in a mixture, which can often benefit from a grouping of pictures and frames that mingles old and new styles and materials. Place a modern plastic frame beside an older-looking wooden molding, and they may set each other off attractively. Sometimes an oval frame sits nicely in a group of rectangular ones, giving just the right amount of variation. Try to preserve some visual unity, however, or the result will appear random and chaotic.

When it comes to mats, the scope is unlimited. You can design your mats to fit into a particular room, or to suit a particular group of images. As mats can be changed without harming the pictures, there is plenty of room for experiment.

LIGHTING

If you decide to light your artpiece, you are faced with two alternatives. You can either 'spot' it, by placing an ordinary light or spotlight to shine on it from elsewhere in the room, or you can fix lighting on or near the frame itself.

Traditionally, painters have used natural light, often a skylight or northern light, to work by and many painters still follow this tradition. Ideally, therefore, pictures should be lit by daylight from above or from a northerly direction — in other words, 'soft' daylight — but this is rarely practical. Electric bulbs are available which imitate daylight and some galleries use fluorescent lighting under a casing of pearly plastic; long strips of lights are sometimes set in brackets, either above or below the picture. Such lighting techniques could be used in a large room to highlight oil paintings but are not advisable with glazed pictures, as the glass tends to reflect the light, detracting from the picture.

Most of us, prefer to use normal domestic lighting so that the artpiece blends in with the rest of the room, although, for a special picture, you could make some adjustments. It might be worth buying lighting strips to fit into brackets and attach to the frame itself to look downward or upward at the picture, or you may achieve an attractive effect by fixing a spotlight to the ceiling or wall and directing the light at the picture. If you dislike the harshness of spotlights, position ordinary household lighting, such as standard lamps or table lamps, in such a way that they provide good lighting for the pictures. Specially placed lights and spots can be hidden behind a piece of furniture or among plants. Experiment until you achieve exactly the effect that you want.

Variety of style
The use of different shapes, sizes and types of frame bring this bedroom to life (right). *Because the arrangement is interesting, the eye is led to each picture. By mixing bold frames with unstriking frames that blend with the color scheme of the room, the overall appearance is never overwhelming.*

Lighting and wiring

For more complex arrangements of framed pictures, lighting becomes important. Care must be taken not to beam a light onto a frame in such a way that a deep molding creates a shadow across part of the picture. Wiring should also be kept as invisible as possible. These pictures and free-standing figures (right) have been lit in such a way that wiring is not too obtrusive. The movable spotlights in the ceiling can be adjusted to emphasize different artworks or aspects of a collection.

Uplighters

Pictures can be lit by directing lamps from beneath. Special uplighting units create an even, diffused light, spreading upward and outward. These are sometimes grouped together to produce an area of even light across the top part of a room or gallery.

Spots

Spotlights can be adjusted to create direct or reflected light. These can run on a strip track, attached to or hung below the ceiling. Single spots can be fixed to the wall, ceiling or floor, and can also be bought fixed to a stand. Use them singly or in groups.

Strips

Sometimes an arrangement of framed pictures looks best when lit by one source. For this, a strip of fluorescent lighting is ideal. Light can be directed onto the pictures by deflectors.

Picture lamps

Individual picture lamps can be bought in a variety of sizes and shapes to suit almost every type of picture. A range of styles is available, from antiqued and old-fashioned to modern designs.

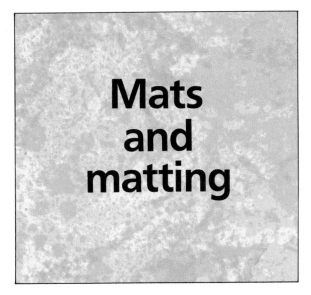

Mats and matting

I t is important to differentiate clearly between the mat — the 'window' which is placed upon the artwork — and the backing card or board onto which the artwork is stuck before the process begins. Confusion arises because this backing is often referred to as the mat. The means by which the artwork is stuck to this backing is also referred to as 'matting.' This section discusses the general principles of mats and matting. The specific techniques are dealt with in clear, detailed, step-by-step terms in the section entitled the Foundation Skills.

THE BREATHING SPACE

Many artpieces are matted as well as framed. In other words, the picture does not make direct contact with the frame but is surrounded by a wide margin which separates the picture from the frame. This is the mat. It is the 'breathing space' between the picture content and the frame itself.

There are no rigid rules governing whether you should or should not have a mat within your frame but, as a basic guideline, consider the artpiece itself: does it, for instance, contain large areas of empty space in its composition, as in the case of a line drawing on a plain white background? This sort of picture would look effective with only a small amount of border, or possibly with none at all. On the other hand, a more crowded picture would benefit from a substantial border of space between the image and the frame.

The mat should be chosen before the frame, because it is the mat that comes next to the artpiece. A great deal of mystery has been attached to the 'proportions' of the mat — the amount of space which should be left at the bottom, sides and top of the image. In fact, the choice is personal and there is nothing magical about the measurements. There are some general rules, however.

The proportions of the mat should not compete with the proportions of the artwork; that is, a big picture does not necessarily need a wide mat and a small picture does not always benefit from having a narrow mat. Generally speaking, a small picture is much improved by a wide mat and a grand-looking frame. Do not follow this principle slavishly or you will end up with a postage-stamp-size picture in the middle of a poster-size mat! There are some exceptions. Small photographs can sometimes look good with narrow mats. A flamboyant modern print can benefit from a wide mat. The result is usually more effective if you avoid giving the visual impression that you have used exactly the same area for the mat as for the artpiece.

There is one important visual illusion which needs

Mat widths
The width of the mat has an immediate effect on the framed picture as a whole. If the mat is too small, it can give the picture a cramped and restricted look. An equal all-round width works well with some images. If the mat is large in comparison with the picture, it is usually better if the picture 'sits' high up in the frame—make sure the mat margin at the bottom of the picture is deeper than that of the other three sides.

Choosing a color
The landscape (top) is painted in muted, earthy colors. With a picture like this, it is usually advisable to choose a color that harmonizes with the subject. The light beige mat makes the picture look darker; the dull olive green immediately picks out the green tones in the composition; black emphasizes the linear content. Sometimes a mat of an unrelated color works: the rich magenta contrasts attractively with the greens and browns in the picture. A picture in bright, expressionistic colors (above) poses a very different problem. The mat generally should be as strong and bright as the colors contained in the painting. The red, blue, yellow, pink and mauve mats all emphasize these particular colors in the portrait. The lime green provides a contrast, the white mat is effective because it picks out the background of the picture, giving a light, spacious feel.

Assembling block frames
For a neat finish, block frames can be edged with wooden strips and clips screwed into these. The framer (right) is using acrylic clips, which do not intrude upon the image. These clips are also available in brass and stainless steel.

Alternative clips
Spring clips (top) and metal corner pieces (above) are found in most framers' supply shops.

to be considered. If the width of space around an artpiece is equal, then the bottom will appear smaller than the other margins. Therefore, an impression of symmetry is best produced by having the space at the bottom a little larger than the other margins — between $1/4$ inch and $3/4$ inch is enough in most cases, depending on the size of the artpiece.

THE BASIC MAT

Matting card is available in three different thicknesses: 4-sheet (1000 microns), 6-sheet (1250 microns) and 8-sheet (1900 microns). 6-sheet is the most commonly used and available in the widest variety of colors: maroon, saxe blue, green, grey, pompadour, pale green, holly green, Russian green, mid grey, bottle green, sepia, seal, coffee, ivory and poster black. 8-sheet is the thickest of the three. Thicker card is available but is quite often difficult to obtain and you will probably have to resort to sticking thin pieces of card together if you want to achieve a thick mat. A thick mat is necessary if you wish to create a deeper recess for your picture. For example, if you are working with a very small image and you want to exaggerate its smallness, fragility or preciousness, you might want a deeply recessed effect.

Block Mats

With modern photographs, a popular method is to use a 'block' mat in which the image juts out to meet the viewer instead of receding inside a 'window' as is usually the case. Block matting is inexpensive and simple to do. The photograph can be trimmed first to remove any white edge. Then it is fixed onto a platform, or block, usually of chipboard or wood, which can be hung as it is or stuck onto a flat surface to leave a surround.

CO-ORDINATING THE COLORS

As with space, the colors of mat and artpiece should not compete with or equal each other. The color of the mat should not overpower or merge with the colors in the picture. On the whole, the colors of the mat should not be too strong or bright but should be muted and neutral.

Sometimes, contrast can be effective: warm colors in a picture can be offset by a cool color in the mat, and vice versa. For instance, a sepia drawing can be enhanced by a gray, pale blue or pale green surround. Traditionally, watercolors are given cool-colored mats, perhaps because of their mainly delicate washes and subjects, although in recent years dark green and brown have become popular, especially for landscapes. The darker the mat, the more quickly the eye is drawn towards the picture.

With many modern prints, the rules of co-ordination are discarded in favor of dramatic effect and instant impact. Bright colors can often successfully surround a modern print to produce a startling and eye-catching effect.

Mats are usually made from matting card. This is available in a variety of colors but, if you are seeking an unusual color or a different pattern or texture, it is quite possible to buy plain white card and stick colored or hand-decorated paper onto it.

If you are using acid-free conservation board — for instance, for an old map or document — you may find that this is available in only white or off-white. Again, you can stick a good quality paper — that is, a hand-made paper produced from rags, which is relatively free from impurities — onto an acid-free board. Do not use the usual spray adhesive or commercial glues in this case; you must buy acid-free tape from an art store or make your own paste from wheatflour and water, otherwise the chemical glue fumes may damage the picture.

WINDOWS

On deciding to use a mat, you are not limited to a single rectangle for the window. You can, if you wish, 'trim' your picture — without actually cutting it — by placing a differently shaped window on top of it. Or you can simply use a window which suits the shape of the original picture.

One extremely effective way in which to set certain artworks, but a more difficult one to cut, is an oval or round mat. Ovals are particularly attractive for matting vignettes; small pictures which do not have hard edges. Oval and circular-shaped mats are available from art stores in standard sizes.

If you require a specific size which is not available ready-cut, and you do not have access to an oval mat cutter, then it is best to hand-cut ovals and circles, using a scalpel or art knife — and great care. You may need considerable practice with scraps of card before you are ready to cut the final piece but other devices are available, such as compass-cutters and templates.

For the adventurous and the skilled, it is possible to cut an endless variety of window shapes. You do not have to follow any particular traditions, although bizarre shapes can look rather ridiculous unless they are particularly suited to the picture and are well designed. It is advisable to use thin card

rather than matting board, at least until you become more skilled and confident.

An artwork can be made to look richer and more expensive by setting it in a double mat, cutting an inner mat which fits under the main one, so that only a small part of the inner mat shows. This small band can be more adventurous than the main mat, perhaps using a bright color or even gilt. A third mat can be added, although care is needed in the choice of color and size — too many confusing edges tend to detract from the artwork.

If you have a collection or series of small artpieces that go well together, they can be set within the same frame. This is called a multiple mat. Two, three, four, six or eight pictures can best be matted together. This obviously takes a little planning and the layout requires thought. It is advisable to set out the pictures on a piece of paper and then to cut windows from the paper. Use this paper pattern as a guide for the final mat.

THE BEVELED EDGE

Almost all mats are cut with a beveled edge. Instead of cutting a piece of board or card with the knife held vertically, the cutting edge is sloped. Thus, instead of a sheer 'canyon' effect, the picture is placed in a window which has inclining sides. This means that no unwanted trace of shadow will appear, and the eye will be brought directly to the picture without hindrance from a hard edge.

Ready-made mats
Ready-made mats (below) are available in a variety of shapes, sizes and colors. Buy mats made from rag fibers — those containing wood pulp can cause staining.

Multi-window mats
An attractive display can be created by using multi-window mats (right). There is no set number of windows that should be cut in a single card, but spacing is crucial and you should try various arrangements before cutting. Pictures that relate to each other can often be visually linked in this way.

Beveled edges
Cutting a beveled edge requires practice, and it is best to experiment first on scraps of card. Keep the knife at a constant angle when cutting. It is essential to have a really sharp scalpel or knife.

Bought mats
Mats can be bought in a rich variety of finishes. In this collection, pale, thin washes contrast with ribboned and marbled borders.
1 *Blue and gold French wash mat.*
2 *Peach and gold English wash-line mat.*
3,5,7 *Line, gold line and wash mats.*
4,6,8 *Marbled mats with contrasting overmats.*
9,10 *Marbled mats with colored undermats.*
11 *Blue-gray marbled mat.*
12 *Taupe marbled mat.*
13 *Cream marbled mat.*
14 *Gold line and wash.*
15 *Green wash.*
16 *Reverse-bevel double mat.*
17 *Marbled mat.*
18 *Yellow wash mat.*
19 *Grey wash mat.*
20 *Pink wash mat.*
21 *Blue wash mat.*
22 *Pink wash mat.*
23 *Line-and-wash mat.*
24 *Marbled mat with contrasting overmat.*
25 *Mulberry paper mat with ribbon inlay.*
26 *Line-and-wash mat.*
27 *Marbled mat with contrasting overmat.*
28 *Line-and-wash, two-tone mat with inlay.*

Beveling evenly by hand is quite difficult. Again, practice is the answer and an extremely sharp cutting tool is vital. Use a metal ruler fixed in position to guide your hand when cutting such an edge. It is possible to obtain a mat cutter, a tool which holds replaceable blades in position, *(see page 54)* but this tool is difficult to get used to and it can take just as long to learn how to use it as to become proficient in cutting by hand.

A fine finishing touch can be given to a beveled edge by gilding it or painting it in a contrasting color.

LINES AND WASHES

There is a refinement which can be added to the process of matting to give the finished product a genuinely period touch. Lines and washes became popular in Europe during the eighteenth century and the technique is known as French matting — an arrangement of lines, sometimes filled with a light wash, set around the picture. The point of the arrangement is to guide the eye gently in to the painting or drawing.

Colors are crucial to this process. They must be chosen carefully to complement those in the picture itself. A common mistake is to make them too brash. The secret is to 'understate' rather than 'overstate.' Otherwise, you will find that when you view the finished product, you notice the lines instead of the picture, which defeats the whole purpose.

Lines and washes work best on a neutral-colored mat, one which does not challenge the arrangement. If you have only a dark-colored or soiled mat, cover it with watercolor paper before applying lines and washes. The lines themselves are often drawn in gold, producing the luxurious effect which has been traditionally popular. Many people will have frequently looked at watercolors surrounded by lines and washes, without noticing that the technique has been used. This is because it has been done with subtlety.

The use of lines and washes became common in Europe towards the end of the eighteenth century and was still popular in the nineteenth. This was when the classical school of English watercolorists came into its own, reaching great heights with such artists as John Sell Cotman (1782–1842) and Thomas Girtin (1775–1802). The lines and washes employed on the mats for their pictures have become so familiar, and are so subtly done that we scarely notice them.

Framers still rely on the line-and-wash method when they want to give an extra finish to the product. The method, although traditionally used with neutral colors by the watercolorists, is nowadays sometimes used on vibrant, modern prints. In this case the line and wash is often bolder, using brighter colors for both the wash and the lines.

One of the attractive features of the line-and-wash technique is that you are not limited. You can vary the width of line, the space between the lines

Line-and-wash borders
An English Lady *by Hans Holbein (above)* has a line-and-wash border, which is painted onto the picture itself. Modern lines and washes include: **1** silver, white, gold and red on light gray; **2** silver and light gray on Wedgewood blue; **3** black, gold and white on cream; **4** Ocher edged with gold, with a fine black line.

Fabric coverings
Mats and frames can be covered by an enormous variety of materials. Velvet, leather, silk, burlap — there is a host of different textures and patterns to choose from. They can be used to cover the outer frames or mats, which will add a dash of color to the artpiece. Spend time experimenting with fabrics, placing them beside pictures to see how they work. Learn how to enhance a picture without overwhelming it. For a less dominant tonal or textural effect, fabrics can also be used for just part of a frame or mat, limited, for instance, to the borders.

and the number of lines. You also have a choice of color. You can use only one color, or you can be adventurous and use several.

Do not launch into the technique without careful preparation. You will need to practice first: try using a mat wash kit (available from art stores) to begin with if you are unused to painting with watercolors. Traditionally, an ordinary nibbed pen was used and craftsmen developed great skill in keeping the lines even and in varying their width, by making confident movements with the pen and ensuring that it did not run out of ink at a crucial time, producing an uneven or broken rule.

Today, we are much luckier. Ruling pens are easily available from art and graphic suppliers; these have adjustable nibs, so that the same pen can be used whatever sort of line you are making. The pen is specially made so that the nib effectively acts as a tiny reservoir to ensure a smooth flow of ink.

COVERING A MAT

Mats can be covered with a variety of materials, not only to produce different colors but to give a variety of textural effects. Two of the most popular materials are burlap and linen, easily obtainable from fabric stores. Matting card can be bought already covered with canvas, burlap or silk but in this case the beveled edge remains uncovered. Fabric of this kind is also often used to cover the wooden insert of a frame for oil or acrylic paintings to give a suitably textured area between the frame and the painted surface.

A fabric mat can also be used to put a picture in context. For example, an early twentieth-century silhouette or an old portrait photograph could be given a period flavor by using taffeta or shot silk on the mat. Black or deep red velvet could be effective in giving a luxurious feel to a grand picture or to lend distinction and formality to a collection of medals or coins, and a suede or leather mat makes a treasured photograph more enduring and special. Many modern pictures are enhanced by the addition of a mat covered in a soft textural weave, such as burlap, canvas or linen. Artists' canvas comes in a range of subtle tones from off-white to a muted dark beige.

Paper, too, has its different textures. Shiny and metallic surfaces can be used as surrounds. In some cases, why not use textured wallpaper? Many people underestimate the amazing variety of patterns available nowadays in paper. Particularly interesting are the unusual, though sometimes expensive, papers used in the bookbinding craft. These include many beautiful marbled patterns and some intricate designs, subtle enough to be useful to the picture framer.

WET AND DRY MATTING

As well as deciding on the mat, you must ensure that the artwork itself is stuck firmly onto a backing. Frequently, the works that you wish to frame will not have been executed directly onto paper thick or

If you intend covering a frame or mat with wallpaper, make sure that it blends with the furnishings of the room. A wallpaper-covered frame or mat can look extremely attractive on a plain wall. The examples shown here include mats that offset the molding, and more exotic cases in which the paper covers both the mat and the molding.

firm enough to support them without this backing material being added before the artwork is taped to the backing board. Remember that if you are dealing with valuable, old or treasured pictures or documents, acid-free conservation board should be used.

The methods used by craftsmen for sticking the picture to a stiff card or board are known as 'wet matting' and 'dry matting.'

Wet matting simply means gluing a picture onto a board, but this has to be done with great care — it is all too easy to end up with bubbles or ridges, and a treasured picture can be ruined.

First a piece of board or card is cut to exactly the same size as the artwork itself. Then an adhesive, preferably a rubber- or plastic-based glue, is brushed smoothly or sprayed evenly on top and the picture carefully positioned. To smooth out the bubbles and any excess glue, it is flattened with a roller or cloth, moving towards the edges from the center. It is advisable to clamp the picture and backing between boards while the glue is drying.

A more permanent professional finish is achieved by dry matting. A sheet of adhesive wax film (available from art and craft stores) is carefully placed between the picture and its backing and the film is then heated to fuse the picture or print to the backing card, giving a perfect product. Professionals use dry-matting presses but these are expensive. Dry matting can be done just as effectively by using a regular household iron.

TAPING

If the picture is stiff enough without a backing, or if you do not want to take the irretrievable step of fusing the artpiece to the backing, use tape. Strips of fabric or masking tape should be used, rather than normal transparent tape, as they can be unstuck comparatively easily.

Very narrow tape is usually sufficient for this process. It can be positioned so that it overlaps both the edge of the picture and the backing card, or — if you do not want to stick it onto the top surface of the picture or print — you can fold the tape back onto itself as you would with stamps in an album, creating a double-sided adhesive tape effect. Double-sided tape is not a wise alternative: as with clear tape, it is too firmly adhesive and can cause difficulties should you wish to remove the artwork at a later date. It is also more difficult to position the artwork correctly using double-sided tape.

HINGE MATS

One way of ensuring that you position an artpiece exactly in place on a backing is to construct a hinge mat. Simply hinge the backing onto the window and close them together, placing the artwork in between the two *(see pages 58–61 for details)*. One advantage of this method is that the window mat and backing are fixed permanently in relation to each other, allowing you to move the picture around on the inner backing until you have found exactly the right position for it.

Types of molding

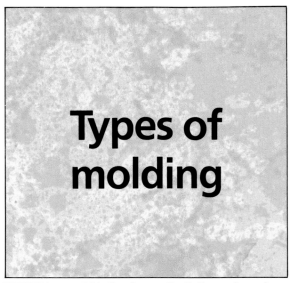

The mold is the frame itself, the outer edges that most people have in mind when they think of a frame. Molding is available in· the form of strips of wood similar to the carved pieces that surround many doors and windows. This section discusses the types of molding available for making your own frames, and the variety of finishes you can apply to them. Specific details on the techniques of measuring, cutting, gluing and finishing frames are given in clear, step-by-step format in the section called Foundation Skills.

There are two types of molding: framers' molding and builders' molding. The main difference between the two is that framers' molding comes with a fitted rabbet; that is, it is 'stepped' in order to allow the picture, mat and glass to fit neatly into place without falling right through the frame.

Builders' molding is primarily intended for trimming doors, windows, baseboards and for other interior finishes. Its use as picture-framing material is incidental and, consequently, it does not have a fitted rabbet.

Consequently, if you use builders' molding, you will either have to cut out the step or create a recess by sticking a narrow strip of wood underneath the molding.

The other important difference is the price. Framers' molding is very expensive. It comes pre-finished and is often made of hardwood. However, for the amateur, it is advisable to use framers' molding initially despite the extra cost because the added complication of having to make rabbets is something that can well be left until you have more frame-making experience.

Once you have a little experience, you may want to use builders' molding. At this stage, when you visit a builders' yard or timber shop, you will probably be surprised at the wide variety of moldings available. Many can be used as picture frames and sometimes two or more types can be put together to make a more elaborate frame.

When browsing through the yards and stores for builders' framing, bear in mind the width of the framing you will need — the picture should not be overshadowed. For a classical or traditional oil painting, a heavy molding several inches wide is desirable; for a more abstract design, a simpler edging is preferable.

One advantage of using builders' molding is that it gives a free range to home experts who wish to create their own finishes.

FRAMERS' MOLDING

Ready-made framers' molding is available in a variety of types and finishes and is to be found in art shops and picture-framing suppliers. There is an impressive array of moldings from reproduction, antique-looking and highly decorated edgings to plain and simple styles.

Framers' moldings include, at the exotic end of the range, the period moldings, gilded and ornate, with delicate leaf-like patterns and elegant and formal ribbed designs reminiscent of the flamboyant courts of the *Ancien Régime* in eighteenth-century France. Also to be found are the more mundane, but attractive, spoon or scoop shapes in which the edging appears as if it has been scooped out regularly right along its line. Related to these are the traditional 'window frame' styles which 'step down' in gentle progression toward the picture. Less expen-

Reproduction frames
From the simple to the extremely ornate, this selection gives an indication of the enormous range of reproduction framers' moldings available today. They are known as: 1 *'Marlborough';* 2 *Red and gold;* 3 *'Van Huysum';* 4 *Red crackle;* 5 *Reproduction seventeenth-century;* 6 *'Rondo';* 7 *'Ripple';* 8 *Gilt Art Nouveau;* 9 *Black and gold;* 10 *Reproduction sixteenth-century Florentine;* 11 *Gilt;* 12 *'Whistler';* 13 *'Edgar Enigma';* 14 *Faux tortoiseshell;* 15 *'Aschkar';* 16 *'Old Ornate Bourlet';* 17 *'Klanaris';* 18 *Golf leaf on blue, no 11;* 19 *'Rembrant';* 20 *Dutch veneer, no 6;* 21 *'Marco 1';* 22 *Gilt;* 23 *Red, black and gold;* 24 *Crackled green and bronze;* 25 *Gold leaf;* 26 *'Jap 1';* 27 *'Chinzan';* 28 *Hogarth;* 29 *Gilt;* 30 *Black Flemish-style.*

Variety of moldings
Builders' molding comes in a surprising amount of different styles. Become more familiar with the range by browsing in lumber yards. Most lumber yards have charts giving a "to scale" range. You will need to make your own rabbet.

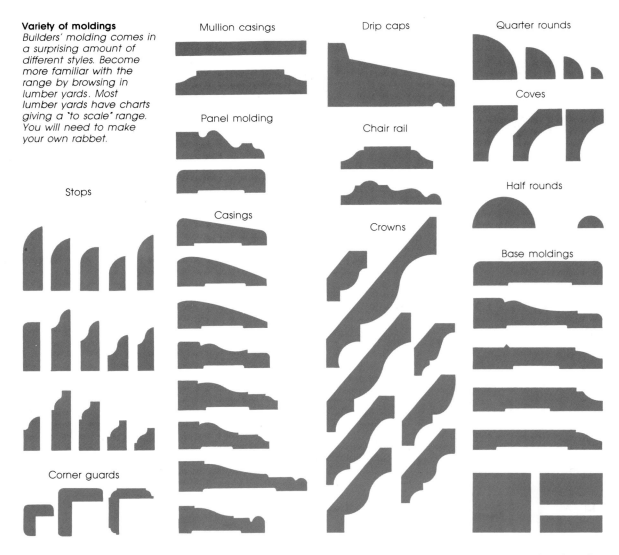

Mullion casings

Drip caps

Quarter rounds

Panel molding

Chair rail

Coves

Stops

Casings

Half rounds

Crowns

Base moldings

Corner guards

sive are the simple wood slopes and flat edges with aluminum finishes.

If you want a metal frame, it can usually be purchased in the form of straight metal strips. However, metal is more difficult to use than wood and special equipment is needed to drill and saw it *(see page 75)*. It is possible to obtain framers' molding which is covered in a thin veneer of metal. This looks like solid metal but can be sawn and treated like any other molding.

One of the more striking characteristics of the range of framers' moldings available is the large variation in width. Here, keen judgment is necessary. Try to keep in mind the artpiece you are framing when looking over the strip of molding.

Insert moldings are also available from picture-frame suppliers. They can be fitted inside the outer frame to give endless combinations of color, shape and texture.

Much variation is provided, too, by different types of wood, each with its own characteristic appearance. One favorite is walnut but you will also find

such woods as maple and cherry prominent on the shelves. Further alternatives include moldings that have been stained, gilded, colored or waxed.

BUILDERS' MOLDING
At first glance there seems to be less variety of builders' molding than framers' molding but great scope is available in the way builders' molding can be combined and finished.

This is not so unusual as it may appear, for, if you look closely at the framers' moldings available, you will often find that they themselves comprise subtle combinations of differently shaped strips.

One common type of builders' molding found in the timber yards and some hardware stores is the heavy, traditional carved strip often found around door frames. This automatically suggests itself for a picture in the grander style, such as a substantial oil painting; but with care and good finishing, some surprising effects are achieved by using this heavy style as a surround for a smaller image, such as a portrait. This can produce the effect of a dramatic

Building up a molding
You can construct your own more elaborate moldings by buying separate strips and assembling them to your own design. For instance, the strips illustrated (above) in cross section were used to create all the moldings at right.

Molding can often be attractively carved. Use existing frames for inspiration and keep the designs simple and tools very sharp.

recess, almost as if you are looking at the picture down a tunnel.

The door moldings and the slightly smaller window strips are the obvious choices; they already look like most framers' moldings. However, there are more unusual styles, such as symmetrical moldings, where the inside edge is the same as the outside one, and rounded or beveled beadings.

With builders' moldings, if the exact profile you had in mind is not manufactured, then you can often come very close to it by combining two or more simpler pieces. If you can persuade your timber merchants' to give you waste pieces or offcuts with which to experiment in different combinations, you will soon become quite expert.

We should stress again the major difference between framers' and builders' moldings — framers' strips come with a fitted rabbet, builders' moldings do not. Whichever molding you choose, you must bear in mind the need for a rabbet. If the basic molding is wide enough you could, perhaps, make a rabbet by gouging it out of the same piece but this is complicated and can lead to mistakes. By far the simplest method is to stick a plain strip of wood to the back of the selected molding (see page 78).

SELECTING THE FRAME

By using an appropriate style of frame you can set off your picture to advantage. When choosing a frame, bear in mind the period and style of the picture. A delicate Japanese print, for example, would not be complemented by a heavy European frame with an eighteenth-century look. Such a mismatch of styles would immediately jolt the senses.

However, selecting a frame is still more a question of personal taste than rules. For instance, many Impressionist and Post-impressionist paintings, their colors brighter and brushwork bolder than that of their predecessors, still look well inside the ornate

Bought frames and moldings
A fine, grained frame with a raised inner edge stands complete at the top right of this selection. The group of grained woods and veneers illustrates the range of frames and moldings available. At the bottom left-hand corner are two types of frame for an oval picture, including a gold slip oval that would enhance a particularly treasured period miniature. A more formal style of room cries out for the more formal, polished frames that are typical of those grouped together

here. Among the narrower frames is an elegant tortoiseshell and gold, two sides of which, are illustrated at the top left. Next to it is a corner piece in antique walnut veneer. Some solid and grand frames lie across the center of the group, including one with fan-shaped wooden inlays. Take care when choosing frames of this sort— consideration should be given not only to the type of picture to be framed, but also to the suitability of the frame to the environment where the picture will hang.

Colorful paint finishes
Some highly decorative paint finishes are featured in this group of moldings. All ready-cut frames, they combine a traditional period flavor with modern experimental finishes. The yellow marbled frame across the center is frankly faked. Yet the result is a tasteful version of a traditional marbling technique, even though the colors are chosen to blend well with a modern interior. It contrasts strongly with the simple green and turquoise ovals that lie next to it in the group. To their bottom right is a series of *specimens including a 'faux' or 'made' (imitation) malachite, and two elegant and narrow samples finished in stippled red and sponged blue. At the extreme top left of the whole group is a marbled dark blue frame, followed by frames sporting a variety of decorative finishes, including two rectangles with painted motifs and decoration over white and green stippled backgrounds.*

gilded moldings of the seventeenth and eighteenth centuries.

Most old pictures look best in their original frames but, of course, this is often impossible to achieve, for the original is frequently missing or hopelessly damaged. The search is then on for a molding that is a modern reproduction of an older look. If possible, the final choice should maintain the original balance: the right proportions between picture and frame, colors that do not clash, and a weight that is not overbearing.

A heavy molding — a massive look — may be suitable for an image such as a portrait, where the head usually takes up most of the picture surface, but it would be inappropriate for a picture containing many small figures or shapes and a lot of space.

Do not overlook the feelings of the artist. Painters often design and paint the frame as well as the picture. The Pointillist, Georges Seurat (1859–91), extended his 'optical' method of mixing colors used in his pictures to some of his frames, creating a total effect.

It is not easy to decide what sort of moldings the artist would have wished for a particular painting but some sensitivity and exploration is called for.

Double Frames

Smaller artworks especially can be set off well by double framing, in which a second frame, or 'slip,' is inserted within a broader one. The terminology varies but we shall refer to these internal frames throughout the book as 'inserts.'

Why use inserts? They provide a broad ribbon of material between the artwork and the outside world and they do it more gently than would a solid wedge-like frame. The insert provides a gentle transition from the artwork to the outside frame and, in turn, the surrounding environment. More than one insert can be used, giving a multiple frame. They can be made of different materials, can be covered with fabrics such as velvet or canvas, and can be veneered or painted.

The color and texture of the insert should harmonize with the artpiece, picking up some of its characteristics. A block of dull red in a picture, for instance, can be reflected by a similar color for the insert. Some purists argue that framers can wrongly emphasize a color or element in the artpiece by reflecting this in the frame, and certainly with some artworks it may be better to use a more neutral tone,

which does not visually alter the artwork. This is a field in which the framer can have fun learning and experimenting with different effects.

Platform Frames

Another alternative for the smaller artpiece is a platform frame. The artpiece is matted onto a larger surround, so that it is physically raised up above the surface. The surround can be made of practically any material but wood or cork are favorites, as they allow the picture to 'breathe.'

A VARIETY OF FINISHES

You, too, can paint your own frames, or you can finish them with other materials and techniques. Framers' moldings are bought ready-finished but builders' moldings allow you to develop your own artistic talent.

Five basic methods of finishing — waxing, staining, texturing, gilding, and painting — are discussed below with special emphasis on painting, which includes such techniques as marbling and spattering. Details on how to effect these techniques are given on pages 86–97.

Waxing

This finishing technique makes the most of the appearance of the wood itself, whether it is soft or hard. Waxing enriches the natural color of the wood and also brings out the grain.

Either apply wax straight to the wood surface or use it as a final finish by waxing over another finish, such as staining. Paint the wax on with a brush; several coats can be used and each one should be polished and buffed up with a soft cloth.

For the most effective wax, mix equal parts of melted beeswax, pure turpentine and pure linseed oil. As an alternative to merely enhancing the color of the wood, you can add your own coloring by mixing wax with artists' oil paint.

Staining

One of the great advantages of staining today is that you are no longer restricted to the traditional, natural colors of wood. Stains are now made in a wide variety of colors and if a store does not stock exactly the shade you require, mix your own.

Staining preserves the patterns of the wood, simply adding color. It does leave the wood porous, however, and you will therefore need to seal the finished piece with a wax or varnish.

Some stains are water-based and some solvent-based: be careful not to mix the two types.

Texturing

There are two basic ways of creating a textured surface. You can either cut into the wood, usually with a pointed instrument or 'raking' tool such as a comb, or you can build up a texture by applying certain substances and working on them.

One such substance is a thick coat of paint. Drag

Velvet slip
Traditional materials have been chosen here for a traditional subject. The needlework has been

placed in a mahogany frame with an insert or slip frame which has been covered in rich green velvet.

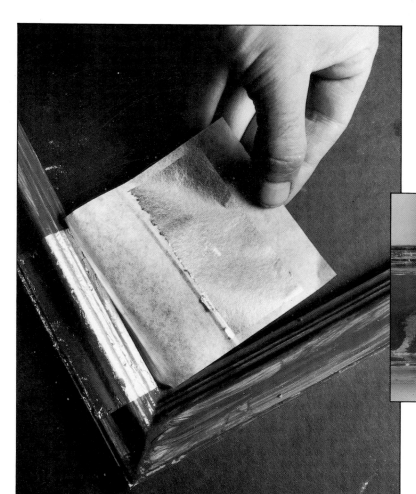

Applying gold leaf
For both these finishes, begin in the same way by giving the basic frame several coats of gesso and bole. The less expensive method of gilding (left) is transfer gilding, which is bought in the form of gold sheets on a paper backing. Water gilding (below) is an old craft, requiring practice and the right equipment.

a comb or other instrument through the still slightly wet paint to create a pattern. Vinyl paint is particularly well suited to this technique. You can also use gesso, a fine plaster-type finish mixed into a paste from powder and water. Experiment with other materials to achieve interesting or unusual results.

Professional Gilding

Gilding, or 'golding' involves covering the surface with a gold color or a very fine layer of real gold. For picture frames, the most expensive and difficult method, but also the most professional, is to use real gold leaf. The word 'real' is used here because you can also buy synthetic gold leaf, although this is harder to apply. Real gold leaf is gold beaten into a sheet only 0.0001mm thick. Bought in books or sheets, it is the result of a craft dating back many centuries. Homer's *Odyssey* contains a passage describing how cattle ready for sacrifice had their horns covered with beaten gold. The process of making gold leaf today has changed little since a German monk wrote a basic outline of the technique in the twelfth century.

There are several different types of real gold leaf, all available from art shops. The main ones are

named after their countries of origin: English, French and Italian. Although they vary in quality, they all tend to be highly expensive. However, real gold leaf applied well provides a beautiful finish.

Water gilding and oil gilding are the two basic methods of applying gold leaf. With water gilding, the gold is burnished to a very bright finish; with oil gilding, the surface is left mat.

Simple Gilding

There are easier ways of achieving a gilt finish on your picture frame than using real gold leaf. Liquid gold leaf or even gold paint can be used for small areas, such as a narrow band, or for retouching.

Metallic powders are widely available: mix them with a varnish. They are especially good for painting motifs and stenciling patterns but if used for larger areas they tend to look streaky and patchy. Powders can be bought for silver and bronze effects as well as gold.

Another material that can be used for gilding is transfer gold. Similar to gold leaf but easier to apply, transfer gold is a thin layer of gold which is purchased on backing paper. Use it like a traditional transfer, but only for smaller jobs.

Creative finishes
Some wooden frames can be painted so that they resemble different materials, such as the apparent marble (right). The painted golden and auburn tortoiseshell (above) is more obviously stylistic. The effect of wood grain can also be created with paint (above right).

Paint Effects

A wealth of finishes can be obtained with paint, using various tricks to produce different effects.

Paint can be used to achieve a surface that resembles a more expensive texture, such as marble, tortoiseshell, or a rare and exotic hardwood. Once you have learned the techniques, you will be amazed at how easily you can obtain a finish that has the look of a highly professional product. A brief summary of paint techniques follows; for more details on how to effect them, see pages 92–97.

Marbling is the technique of using broken color to capture the effect of the irregular streaks of the seams in real marble. It rarely actually deceives but marble is accepted today as a legitimate pattern in its own right.

Wood-graining is one of the older crafts. Victorian decorators became skilled at producing the effect of wood grain on furniture and only a few years ago examples of it could still be found in many homes.

Apply a thin layer of paint, so thin that it is transparent, and then carefully drag a dry brush over it to achieve a wavy texture. On top of this, while the paint is still wet, scratch in lines to represent the grains of wood.

Tortoiseshelling makes use of oil-based paint, which is painted into a textured varnish and smoothed out to create the subtly blurred surface of real tortoiseshell.

Rubbing back consists of painting a wet paint onto a dry one of a different color. Wipe the second color while it is still wet to leave just a few traces in the grains of the wood. Rubbing back is particularly effective when using gold over a warm color such as red, or silver over a cool color or black.

Vinegar painting is sometimes called putty graining. It creates a grain-like pattern but does not attempt to imitate real wood and is most effective when bright colors are used. Any pattern can be pro-

Etched patterns
A combination of gilding, gesso and paint can give spectacular effects (left). The gesso is etched or scoured with a sharp implement and the gilding and color applied on top.

Spattering with a brush
Spattering gives a speckled effect (above): use bright colors for a modern effect, or neutral or black to create an antique look.

duced using this technique. Paint one color onto the frame and allow it to dry. Then paint on a second color made as a paste from vinegar, sugar, powder color and a little detergent. While it is still wet, dab it with cork or crumpled paper to make a pattern.

Flicking and spattering require a stiff brush, such as a toothbrush. Run your thumb along the bristles or hit the handle on a strip of wood to spatter the paint onto the molding. If this is done in a restrained way, using a neutral color, you can make gilt finishes look old and more subdued. Alternatively, you can let rip and use lots of colors on top of each other to create an exciting effect.

Patinas can be used to create subtle warm and cool tones on the same frame. Begin with a basic pale gray base. Then apply cooler or warmer grays in a thin wash. To make a cooler gray, add blue to the basic gray; for a warmer tone, add burnt sienna or yellow ocher. The best effects are made by mixing warm and cool tones. Apply two or more transparent glazes of warm and cool tones, allowing each layer to dry before applying the next.

Matching the frame to the artpiece can be done with a plain matching color, mat or high gloss, or you can decorate the molding in a way which is visually sympathetic to the artwork. This is a very old practice: the man generally credited with having discovered oil painting, Jan Van Eyck (1390–1441), is known to have painted his frames to match his pictures. Care is needed, but with flair and imagination frames can be decorated in a way that does not impose an incongruous or overbearing style on the original picture.

Antiquing — making a frame look older and toning down brash colors — can be achieved by using some of the methods mentioned above. Spattering, for instance, if done with black or a dull color, can tone down a harsh surface. Or rubbing back can be used, again with a dull, neutral top color.

The Basics of Framing

Materials and Equipment

▪

The Foundation Skills

▪

Finishing Techniques

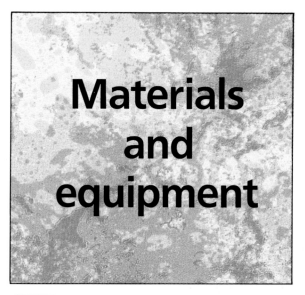

Materials and equipment

Before you embark on framing a piece, it is essential to become familiar with the parts that make up a framed artpiece and their roles, and to purchase the right tools and equipment. This section takes you through the basic parts of a frame and describes the range of equipment you will need to complete a variety of frames.

PARTS AND FITTINGS

From the outside looking inward, a framed artpiece is made up of a **rabbeted molding**, **glass**, a **mat**, the picture, **inner backing**, and **backing board**. These are all held in position by **brads** or **veneer pins** and the framed picture is hung with **hanging fittings.**

The names of parts can be confusing as craftsmen have not always been consistent when giving terms to components and techniques. Detailed below are the terms used for a standard glazed frame with a mat and for the fittings that attach it to the wall.

Rabbeted Molding

You can purchase molding with rabbet already fitted — ie a stepped molding — otherwise you will need to buy a separate strip to fit along the bottom of your molding to make the rabbet.

The back of the rabbeted molding, which rests against the wall, is referred to as the 'bottom edge' or sometimes the 'rabbeted edge.' The side of the molding, which you would see if you pressed your eye against the wall and looked at the side of the frame, is called the 'back.' The front edge of the molding, the strip which the viewer sees, is called the 'front' or 'face.' The edge of the molding, which overlaps the picture slightly is known as the 'sight edge.'

Glass

The pane of glass used for glazing a picture is usually $1/12$ inch thick. A very common commodity, it is stocked by all main glaziers and it can be bought cut to the correct size if you do not wish to cut it yourself.

Non-reflective glass can also be purchased but this is more expensive and many people feel that it does not give the picture the bright look usually lent by glass but a duller more mat appearance. It is, however, entirely a matter of personal taste and many pictures are framed in non-reflective glass.

Acrylic sheet is sometimes used, as this, too, is non-reflective but it is generally not advisable as it scratches easily, becomes static after wiping, attracting more dust, and yellows with age.

Mat

This is a specially made piece of card, which is white all the way through, except for the surface color. This means that when you cut the bevel to make the window for the picture, you are left with a uniform clean white edge.

Inner Backing

This is the stiff card against which the picture itself is either stuck or held firm in some other way.

If the picture is rare or antique, the inner backing will need to be acid-free conservation board, which is obtainable from specialist suppliers.

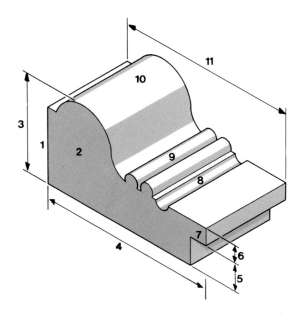

Profile of a molding
1 *Outside molding edge*
2 *Molding profile*
3 *Total molding height*
4 *Total molding width*
5 *Rabbet*
6 *Molding inside edge*
7 *Lip of rabbet*
8 *Fluting*
9 *Beading*
10 *Ridge*
11 *Molding face*

Backing Board and Brads

This is the final backing, usually made of hardboard or craft board and measured to exactly the same size as the glass. After it has been fitted, the tiny gap between it and the bottom edge of the molding is sealed with brown gum strip as a guard against dust.

When the backing board is lower than the bottom edge of the molding, it can be fixed into place with brads.

Sometimes the rabbet is too shallow to accommodate the glass, the mat and the inner backing as well as the backing board. In this case, the brads are tapped into the molding and then bent over so that their heads hold the components in position.

If the hardboard is exactly flush with the back of the frame, it can be either beveled, to allow the brads to be tapped into the molding at an angle, or it can be held in place with turn clips.

Hanging Fittings

Many different types of fittings are available. Screw eyes, which sometimes have a second ring, are the most common. Such rings are attached directly to the bottom edge of the molding. Back hangers are useful when a molding is narrow. These are fixed into the backing board. For bigger pictures with heavy frames, more substantial fittings are required, such as D-rings or otherwise-shaped back hangers. These rings are fitted into a fold of metal, which is screwed into the bottom edge of the molding.

Fittings are usually fixed a third of the way down the picture. Take care to use picture wire of the correct thickness for the weight of the framed picture.

Wall Attachments

In most cases a simple picture hook matched to the weight of the picture will be sufficient to hang it on an ordinary stud-frame wall. However, if the picture is particularly heavy, make sure that the supporting hook is fixed directly into a stud or cross brace fitted between two adjacent studs.

To locate a stud, tap the wall with your knuckle, moving across the wall until you no longer hear a hollow sound. Then make a series of test holes to find the precise position of the stud. Studs are generally placed 16 inches apart from center to center. Two hangers set apart spread the load.

Heavy duty hang rings

Wall fixtures

Lightweight hang rings

Corner strengtheners

Picture plates

Turn clips

Screw on clips for block mats

Spring clips for block mats

Backing board

Artpiece

Mat, can be double or triple; not usually used for oils

Insert

Frame

Glass, not usually used for oils

DIRECTORY OF TOOLS AND EQUIPMENT

Most professional craftsmen regard with horror the old maxim that only a bad workman blames his tools and advise that no work should be undertaken without tools of exactly the right kind and the proper quality. Even if you are not planning anything elaborate, some good basic tools are essential if the job is to be done well. This directory includes all the basic tools and equipment needed for successful picture framing.

Artists' brushes It is useful to have a selection of these for executing oil and acrylic paint finishes.

Backsaw Also known as a tenon saw. Ordinary saws tend to be flexible and bend; the metal reinforcing strip along the top of this saw prevents the saw blade from 'weaving.' It can be fixed to the workbench with screws.

Bole A red clay pigment used especially in water gilding. Bole is painted on the gesso base to provide a soft, satin-like surface for the gold leaf.

Brads Fine, round-wire nails from ½ inch to 2 inches long, brads can be nailed into the corners of a freshly glued frame to provide a more permanent re-inforcement. They have very small heads that can be punched below the surface of the wood. There is also a smaller variety of brad which is useful for very lightweight framing. These tiny nails are sufficient to reinforce the corners of the frame.

Burnisher Needed to make the smooth, shiny finish so characteristic of water gilding. Most burnishers have an ordinary wooden handle and a curved, smooth metal end which is available in different shapes and sizes for different tasks and is used to burnish the leaf onto the frame.

C-clamp If you are making your own rabbet, C-clamps (also known as G-clamps) can be used to clamp the molding to the underlying strip of wood. Also useful as an additional grip.

Carpenters' rule The recommended straight-edge to use when glass cutting. An ordinary thin metal rule is too flimsy to hold the cutter.

Colored paper Useful for covering mat board if the exact color of mat board that you require is not available.

Conservation board Sometimes known as 'museum board,' conservation board has been treated to avoid the tendency of ordinary mat board to absorb acid from the polluted atmosphere, which leads eventually to discoloration of the picture. It is advisable to use acid-free conservation board if you are matting old or valuable drawings or prints.

Craft knife A sharp, general-purpose craft knife, able to cut both card and fabric, is essential for mat cutting. Change the craft blade frequently, especially when you are cutting the beveled edge of a mat, otherwise the finish will be fuzzy.

Decorating brushes It is useful to have a selection of these brushes for waxing, staining and some paint finishes. You will probably not need one more than 1½ inches wide.

Drill Needed to make the pilot holes in the corners of molding pieces before they are secured together. The most suitable type of drill is a portable household power drill but a good hand drill is perfectly

Diamond glass cutter

Wheel glass cutter

Backsaw

Craft knife

G-clamp

Hand drill

adequate. Whichever you decide on, you will need a collection of drill bits.

Dry-matting film Available from graphic suppliers and art shops, this film is placed between the canvas and the backing board and, when heat is applied, fuses the two together.

Dry-matting press Commercial dry-matting presses are usually heavy and inappropriate for home framers. Lighter versions are available which are useful if you intend doing a lot of dry matting; these are basically electric metal presses for use on a table.

Face-pieces These scraps of wood are inserted in the vice and screwed to the jaws to prevent the molding from being damaged by the vice as it is being worked on.

Felt-tipped pen (delible) Can be used to mark the size of the piece of glass required directly onto the glass before cutting. Another method is to draw the cutting lines on a piece of paper, place the paper beneath the glass and follow the lines.

Fitch brushes These are inexpensive and useful for stippling and small-scale decoration and for the spattering effect used in antiquing.

Gesso A gesso base is needed for both water and oil gilding. Mix gesso powder, which is a chalk, with rabbit-skin glue (both available from art stores) to make the gesso or buy it ready-mixed in fluid form.

Gilders' cushion A padded board covered with suede and used for resting gold leaf. A stiff paper screen boxes in one end of the cushion to protect the gold leaf against drafts: the leaf is so fine and

fragile that it can be lifted off the cushion surface by the slightest draft and crumpled, making it unfit for further use.

Gilders' knife This knife has a very fine blade and is used for separating sheets of gold leaf.

Gilders' tip A flat brush with thinly spaced camel hairs, a gilders' tip is stroked across the hand or hair so that it gathers just enough natural oil from the human skin to pick up a sheet of gold leaf from the gilders' cushion.

Glass Picture-framing glass is lighter in weight than normal window glass. It is available in a standard thickness of $1/12$ inch, as opposed to the $1/8$ inch thickness of window glass or the very thick plate glass used in shop windows, which is sometimes as much as $1/6$ inch thick.

Glass cutter There are two types of glass cutter. The one that is easiest for the beginner to use comprises a handle with a steel revolving wheel. Most experienced framers, however, prefer the glaziers' diamond, a handle that holds a diamond, which is especially suitable for thin picture glass. Both are used manually and rely upon good measurement and judgment.

Graining brush This brush has little tufts of bristles for building up layers of grain effect.

Iron If you do not possess a commercial heat press an ordinary domestic iron can be used for small-scale projects to apply heat in the dry-matting process.

Mat boards As picture framing has become more

Dry-matting press

Miter cutter

Miter block

popular, an increasingly large choice of mat boards has come on the market. Almost all of them have the traditional distinction of being white throughout their thickness regardless of outer coloring, so that the beveled edge shows up white. The edge is usually left white but it provides a good base on which to place a gilt strip, or another color, if you wish. Choice of thickness is usually limited to 4-sheet, 6-sheet and 8-sheet board, although thicker card can be obtained or two boards can be stuck together.

Mat cutter This specialist tool cuts the inside beveled edge of the mat at an angle of 45 degrees. The most useful type of mat cutter has a replaceable blade which is held firmly at an angle and can be set to different depths, depending on the thickness of the mat board.

Metal ruler When cutting a straight edge, either with a knife or mat cutter, a metal ruler is essential. If you use a wooden or plastic ruler, you will pare the ruler's edge. A carpenters' metal straight-edge is ideal, if a little more expensive than an ordinary metal ruler.

Miter box Essential for forming the corners of a frame, a miter box must be absolutely accurate. It cuts at an angle of 45 degrees and if it is out of line by even half a degree, the inaccuracy wil be obvious in the finished frame. It is therefore worthwhile buying a good quality miter box. Unfortunately, a miter box may become wobbly with use and therefore lose its accuracy. The simplest sort of miter box is a wooden frame, shaped like an open-ended box with slits in each side to guide the saw at a constant angle of 45 degrees. The box is usually made of hardwood but, even so, continuous sawing can wear away the

precise measurements of the slits. A slightly more expensive version can be obtained with metal reinforcements at the top of the slits.

Miter clamp Once the molding has been cut at right angles for the corners it needs to be held firmly in place so that the pieces can be glued and nailed, and to be gripped in position until the glue has dried. For this, a miter clamp, made of metal and sometimes called a corner clamp, is used. If possible, the clamp should be fixed by clamping it onto the corner of the table or work-bench to give added stability. A simpler type of corner clamp is made of four plastic right angles which fit around the pieces of molding and are tightened by a cord. Both types are suitable for simple framing but, for heavier frames, the metal one is easier to use.

Miter cutter Some of the more sophisticated miter boxes are made entirely of metal, and the most advanced of all is the miter cutter which is a miter box and saw combined in one piece of equipment. These are designed to give absolute rigidity and to prevent the saw from descending too low and causing damage.

Mottling brush Used for breaking up and highlighting the grain.

Oilstone Useful to rub down sharp, newly cut edges of glass.

Paint thinners Useful for cleaning dirty oil paintings and for lubricating a wheel cutter during glass cutting.

Paintbrushes Those cut on the diagonal and

Miter clamp

Vice

normally used for painting awkward angles on windows are useful for painting the crevices in moldings.

Rabbet plane Also known as a rebate or fillister plane, it has an adjustable fence, a depth gage and a cutter that is set in a forward position for planing up to a stopped rabbet.

Sable brushes Usually used by watercolorists, sable brushes are useful for fine finishing.

Sandpaper Essential for smoothing a wooden frame before applying a final surface finish and for rubbing down the layers of gesso as they are applied in both water and oil gilding.

Shellac varnish Whether you have a gesso or bole final surface, an oil-gilding project must be sealed with a coat of shellac varnish.

Spray glue Needed in wet matting to attach the picture to the inner backing as it gives an evenly glued surface.

Table If you do not have a work-bench, a table can be used instead. It must be firm and, if you are setting it up for any length of time, it should be fixed to the floor for extra stability.

Tack hammer A light hammer especially suitable for hammering in the pins and nails used in picture framing. A heavier hammer tends to bend the pins, even if used with care.

Tacking iron For use in conjuction with a dry-matting press, a tacking iron is like a tiny domestic flat iron

but is angled on a handle to enable precision use. It is used to fuse together the picture, dry-matting sheet and inner backing before final bonding.

Try square Essential for drawing accurate right angles when marking out the window in the mat board.

T-square Like the try square, a T-square is useful for marking out accurate right angles.

Turpentine When cutting glass, keep the wheel cutter lubricated by frequently dipping it into turpentine or paint thinners.

Vice An ordinary vice can be used to grip pieces of molding in place while general work is being done on them but its role in picture framing is an all-purpose rather than a specific one. It is also used for drilling and trimming wood, for instance, and should not be confused with the role of the clamp, which is used specifically to hold the corners at rigid right angles.

Wallpaper paste and **water-based glue** Used for wet matting, although because they are water-soluble they are unsuitable for prints and drawings done in non-waterproof inks.

Woodwork glue For gluing the corners of the frame together, a synthetic, PVA-based woodwork glue is most suitable. You do not need to use very much on each corner.

Work-bench Provides a solid and level work surface.

The foundation skills

For oil and acrylic paintings, canvases, hardboard panels or any type of artpiece which cannot be trimmed, the rabbet measurement is usually the most useful as it indicates the total ground area, including that which is hidden beneath the rabbet. Measure the length and the width of the artpiece and mat, if there is one, and then add 1/8 inch all round — this allows for easy insertion of the artpiece into the rabbet. Many canvases used for oil paintings, especially home-made ones, are 'off-square.' If this is the case, add the extra 1/8 inch to the longest measurement.

An oil painting is sometimes fitted very snugly into the rabbet, almost as far as it can go, inevitably hiding some of the image. If it is important not to cover any of the composition, and the image reaches virtually to the edge of the canvas, then it will be necessary to frame the picture with the smallest possible fraction of it hidden behind the rabbet, using spacers to hold it in place, and you will need to take a sight measurement. A sight measurement gives the distance between the inside edges of the front of the frame, indicating precisely the area of the artpiece which will be finally open to view.

WET, OR COLD, MATTING
Some drawings or prints are too flimsy to stand by themselves when being placed between backing board and frame, and need to be stuck fast to a rigid support. Gluing a picture to such a board is called wet matting. Wet matting is also the quickest and simplest method of block matting — fixing an artwork to a platform projecting from the surround.

Paintings executed on canvas, which have been removed from their stretchers, can be wet matted. The technique is also suitable for photographs, drawings, prints and documents and is a good way of preserving something of sentimental value, which

B efore embarking on specific projects, it is necessary to master the foundation skills of picture framing. These fundamental skills are described below in detail, enabling you to tackle with ease any of the projects that follow.

MEASURING THE ARTPIECE
It is important to take precise measurements whether you are measuring the artpiece, the mat or the molding. In fact, it is often worthwhile taking a measurement twice to double check.

Before you can calculate the length of the molding you will need to know one of two basic picture measurements: either the 'rabbet' measurement or the 'sight' measurement.

THE PROFESSIONAL METHODS

The professional methods of framing often differ from the basic picture-framing techniques. Consequently, throughout this section, in addition to the basic techniques of framing, many of the professional techniques are also illustrated and described in step-by-step format. The professional techniques covered are those for:

- Wet, or cold, matting
- Dry, or hot, matting
- Attaching the window mat
- Cutting a beveled window
- Cutting an aluminum frame
- Underpinning
- Assembling an aluminum frame

The diagram (left) illustrates the importance of taking accurate measurements. Whether you have a matted picture or an oil painting on a stretcher, you must fit the artpiece snugly into the rabbet of the frame. The diagram (below) clearly shows the difference between the sight and rabbet measurements. The sight measurement of a framed artpiece indicates the area of the artpiece open to view. The rabbet measurement indicates the total area of the artpiece, including that which is hidden behind the rabbet.

+ ⅛ inch

Rabbeted molding

+ ⅛ inch   Canvas

Matted artpiece

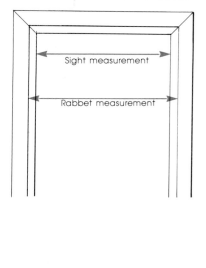

Sight measurement

Rabbet measurement

you would not want creased or torn. However, because it is difficult to reverse, wet matting should be avoided when dealing with antique or rare pictures.

Various types of glue are suitable for wet matting. An aerosol spray glue is most suitable for pictures done on thin papers and any synthetic glue is suitable for those carried out on thicker paper.

Wallpaper size is often a less expensive and just as convenient alternative. Mix this according to the instructions on the package but remember that it is water-soluble, so avoid using it on works of art that are printed or painted using water-soluble materials, as traces of it could soak through. If wallpaper size is applied to plywood, it can cause it to warp. When using wallpaper size, remember to 'pre-size' the board: give it a coat of size and allow it to dry. This will seal the board and prepare the surface for the final sizing, resulting in a better grip.

When using a non-aerosol adhesive, it is common to misjudge the amount needed and place too much glue on the backing, so some practice is advisable. To prevent bubbles appearing when matting a large print or photograph, wet the picture before positioning it on the glued board. Do not try this, however, with a watercolor or a print

effected with water-soluble inks.

When glue and size matting, flatten the artwork, removing any trapped air, by applying pressure with a roller: roll firmly out from the center of the picture — a technique also designed to remove any surplus glue. You can ensure that no glue seeps onto the picture by covering it with a sheet of paper before you start rolling. Alternatively, if only a small print is being matted, or if you do not have a roller, a soft, dry rag can be used: again work outward from the center. It is a good idea to weight the picture onto the glued surface while it is drying. This can be done by clamping the picture and mat between two sheets of plywood, or placing them beneath one or two heavy books.

DRY, OR HOT, MATTING

Dry matting is the process of fusing the artpiece to the inner backing by means of heat and a special adhesive sheet. Place the sheet between the picture and the backing and apply the heat. The sheet will melt, fixing the picture firmly on the backing.

If you intend to carry out a lot of dry matting, it may be worth investing in a press. Place the picture face down on a dry surface while the press is warming up. Position a sheet of matting tissue — the adhesive sheet — so that it covers the picture's reverse side entirely, and fix the picture and adhesive sheet in position by applying a warm tacking iron along one edge. If more than one adhesive sheet is needed to cover the area, ensure that the edges are butted and do not overlap, otherwise creases and bubbles will mar the result. With each new sheet that is added, apply a tacking iron along one edge to fix it into position.

Trim the edges of the adhesive sheet precisely with a very sharp scalpel or craft blade. Turn the picture and sheet face up and position it on the inner backing. Cover the picture with brown paper and apply the tacking iron again to hold the backing fast along one edge. Place the picture and backing in the press, on top of an extra piece of board for additional stability, and position a sheet of protective paper — usually provided with the adhesive sheet — on top. Close the press and leave for between 30 and 60 seconds to fuse. Remove from the press and place the backing, picture and protective paper under a heavy weight, such as a pile of books.

If you do not have a press, a domestic iron is also suitable both for the tacking and the final bonding. Simply follow the above procedure, substituting an iron for the press. Use a solid, flat working surface and set the iron to 'linen.' Iron out from the center for the final bonding.

HINGE MATTING

In a hinge mat, the inner backing and the mat are hinged together. This keeps the mat board and inner backing together during framing, preventing

Spray matting
The advantage of spray matting is that it is easy to apply. Place the artwork face down on a clean surface and spray evenly over the back with spray glue (left). Position the artwork on the matting board—many spray adhesives have a delayed drying time to allow you to adjust the artwork. Smooth down from the center outward (below).

Glues for matting			
Type	**Advantages**	**Disadvantages**	**Drying time**
Wallpaper size	Cheap and strong	Should not be used for valuable items	A few hours to dry properly
Contact glues	Very strong and quick; multi-purpose; can be used on card, rubber, laminates etc	Should not be used for valuable items—once the glued surfaces touch they cannot be pulled apart again.	Instant
Dry mats	Strong; extremely professional finish	Requires heat	Instant
Spray glues	Convenient; allows for adjusting and repositioning	Expensive	Up to a few minutes (some have adjustment times)
PVA (can be diluted with water for sticking paper and card)	Can be used on paper, card and fabric, and is very strong		Half an hour to a few hours (depending on type)
Organic glues (including artists' size)	Good for fabrics, card and paper	It goes off; requires gentle heat—can be 'killed' if overheated	A few hours to dry thoroughly
Latex glues	Good for canvas, card, paper etc	Difficult to remove excess; strong smelling	About one hour

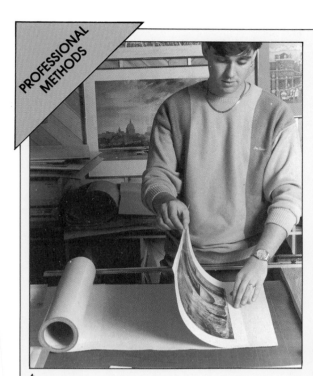

Wet, or cold, matting

1 The picture is placed carefully on pressure sensitive film, which is then detached from the rest of the roll.

2 The backing of the film is then peeled off, leaving a strongly adhesive surface. The picture is now ready to place on the backing. Here, craft board has been used as both inner backing and backing board.

3 One end of the print is pressed down on the backing and passed through the rollers of the matting press. The rest of the picture is held tautly with one hand against the top roller, while the card and picture is gradually wound between the rollers. In this way, no air bubbles are allowed to form. When the entire print has passed through the rollers, the matted picture is wound back through the press to ensure that the print is stuck firmly to the board.

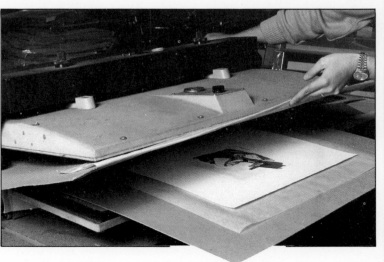

Dry, or hot, matting

Dry matting provides the strongest and most professional-looking bond. The picture is placed face up on dry-mat tissue, which is coated with wax and placed on top of the backing. It is then covered with a piece of clean board to prevent the wax not covered by the picture from sticking to the lid of the press. It is all inserted in the pre-heated dry-matting press and left for 1 minute to fuse.

Hinge mats

1 The first stage in the making of a hinge mat is to fix the picture onto a backing. Attach the artwork to the backing with tape, so that it can be adjusted when the window is fitted over it and can also be removed later if necessary.

2 Cut another mat, exactly the same overall size as the first 'backing' mat and cut out a window.

3 Lay the two mats end to end, and tape them together.

4 Finally, carefully fold the window over the matted picture.

1

2

3

4

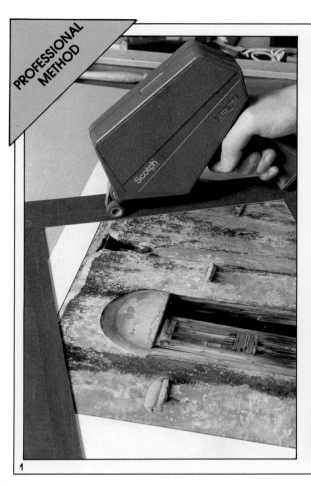

PROFESSIONAL METHOD

Attaching the window mat
1 Double-sided tape is applied to the back of the window along the top and sides, or, if hinge matting, just to the top edge. The mat is never fixed at both top and bottom as this might result in the picture wrinkling if the picture drops. The mat is then positioned on top of the backing and picture.
2 Any additional backing is then cut away with the straight edge of a mat cutter. The window mat is used as a guide to leave a clean edge to the matted picture.

1

2

them from slipping, and allows you to change the artwork and use the same mat over and over again.

To make a hinge mat, cut the window and lay the mat and the inner backing face down on a clean surface, head-to-head with their top edges flush. Then stick the two together, placing a piece of masking tape, brown paper tape or fabric tape at the top of the backing. Next, fit the picture: determine the exact postition of the picture by trial and error, moving it by degrees behind the window. Then stick the picture onto the inner backing by one of two methods: either affix small pieces of tape to its edges, or, if you particularly do not want the surface of the artwork to be touched by tape, fold over a piece of tape into a little hinge and place it behind the artwork. Double-sided tape can also be used but is not recommended because of its fiercely adhesive quality, which makes precise positioning and removal of the artwork difficult.

CONSERVATION MATTING
Although conservation techniques have always been used to help preserve particularly precious artworks, their use has become more common in recent years as attention has been increasingly drawn to the problems of environmental pollution.

Conservation matting is not simply a matter of iso-

lating the picture from the atmosphere, which contains acid particles and other harmful chemicals. The picture must also be separated from the actual frame, for much of the material used in frame making contains traces of acids which might be damaging to a picture over a long period of time. Acid traces can be found in almost all materials, including cardboard, paper and wood, when they are not specifically acid-free.

Conservation matting, therefore, involves selecting acid-free materials and ensuring that these, and no others, are placed next to the artwork. Acid-free matting board, sometimes known as conservation board or museum board, is widely available from specialist suppliers. Acid-free cloth tape can be used to hinge the matting board to the inner backing and rice paper can be used to stick the artwork to the inner backing. Tear the rice paper into strips, fold into hinges and stick them to the inner backing and artwork with an acid-free glue. Cardboard, especially corrugated cardboard, which is sometimes used as backing, should be avoided when conservation is important: its acid content tends to be particularly high. When you have completed the framing, turn the picture upside down and seal the back securely with a paper dust seal. To achieve a tight seal between

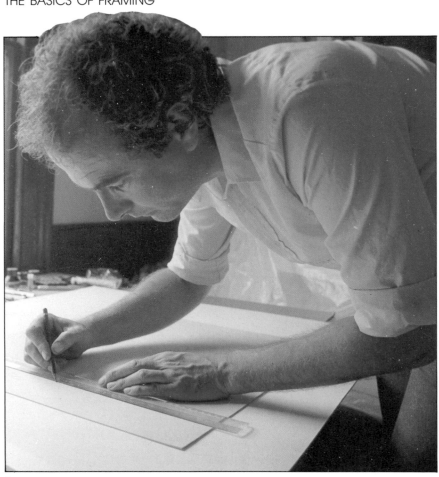

1

Cutting a rectangular mat
1 First, decide on the size of the mat: the borders on either side of the artwork should be of an identical width and the bottom border should be wider than the top border. Cut the total area of mat card required from the whole sheet, ensuring that all the corners are square. Now, with a pencil, mark the widths of the borders at several points along each side. Join the pencil dots on one side with a ruler and pencil in a line. Do the same for the other three sides of the window, overshooting at the corners so that you make clear right angles.
2 Using a protractor or try square, check that the rules of the window form perfect right angles at the corners. Amend the lines if necessary.
3 Place a metal straight-edge along one of the marked lines; tap in two nails at either side of the mat board and rest the ruler against them. Using a sharp craft knife, cut along the straight-edge at a constant angle of 50 or 60 degrees. Repeat for the

2

4

3

5

6

7

other sides of the window.
4 Tidy the corners of the beveled window with the point of the craft knife blade.
5 The adjoining sides of the window should meet in a clean, precise corner.
6 Rub out any pencil marks that are still visible on the mat.
7 An interesting variation of the standard rectangular mat can be made by 'clipping' the top two corners. Mark the diagonal rules on the mat with a pencil before you begin cutting the beveled edges.

the glass and the frame, pack the backing board, mat, artwork and glass tightly and make the seal firm by tacking nails into the rabbet.

MEASURING THE MAT

As a rule, the mat is cut first, and then the frame around it, enabling you to position the artwork in the mat. Usually, the sides and the top margins around the mat are slightly narrower than the bottom margin, so that the artwork sits up high in the mat.

Remember that you are beginning with two pieces of card — the backing card and the mat itself. Unless you are using conservation board, the inner backing can be of a cheaper material than the mat. The inner backing and the mat should be measured and cut so that they both fit neatly into the rabbet.

When measuring the window, place the card face down on a clean surface and mark the measurements on the 'wrong,' ie reverse, side. Decide the width of the mat surround and mark the margins in as lines on the reverse side of the card. The final window measurement can now be checked with a try square for corner squareness, after which it is ready for cutting.

CUTTING A BEVELED WINDOW

A beveled edge — a sloping, rather than straight, edge — gives a professional finish to the window of a mat.

A simple and easily available tool, such as a craft knife, is usually used to cut a beveled edge, and a metal straight-edge is necessary to guide your hand when you are cutting. The blade used for cutting a beveled edge must be absolutely razor-sharp. Always keep a supply of spare blades in stock

Hand cutting an oval with a knife
It is extremely difficult to achieve a neat, clean edge when handcutting ovals, so restrict hand cut ovals to mats that will be covered by paper or fabric.
1 *Using a very sharp scalpel, hold the template down firmly and cut round it.*

1

2 *When you have cut the oval, remove the template and trim any jagged edges. Don't overdo the trimming, however, as this can distort the finished shape.*

2

and as soon as cutting becomes slightly difficult, change the blade. Do not use a wooden or plastic ruler, as the knife will shave small flakes from it, not only blunting the blade but quickly ruining the straight-edge and making the ruler unusable.

After measuring and marking out the window, place the card from which it is to be cut face down on a board or table where it won't matter if the surface is cut or damaged. To lengthen the life of your blade, insert newspaper between the card and the board so that you cut into the newspaper rather than the board or table. To prevent the metal straight-edge from slipping while you are cutting, it is a good idea to tap in two nails — one at each side of the mat board — for the ruler to rest against.

With the card still face down, place the ruler along the first marked line to be cut and insert the knife slightly beyond the corner mark outside the window area. This slight overcut — equivalent in distance to the thickness of the card — will not be noticed on the right side of the mat and will ensure

that the corners are sharp and precise.

There are two alternative methods for the next part of the procedure, both requiring practice. For the first method, cut along the straight-edge in one smooth stroke, keeping the pressure even, and holding the knife at a constant angle of between 50 and 60 degrees. Cut beyond the corner of the line by the same amount as the overcut at the first corner — the thickness of the card. For the second method, lightly score along the line at the correct angle. Then make another scoring stroke along exactly the same line and at the same angle; repeat until you have cut right through the card. After the first line is lightly scored, you might find it more comfortable to do without the straight-edge.

Repeat the cutting procedure for all four sides of the window. The beveled edge should be a smooth, clean slope but if you are left with a few jagged pieces, you can often remove them by carefully rubbing them down with very fine sandpaper or emery-cloth.

1

Using a hand cutter

1 *There are several types of hand cutters on the market. This is a Dexter cutter.*

2 *Make straight cuts by placing the cutter against a metal straight-edge.*

3 *Hold the straight-edge very firmly and draw the cutter along, applying a firm, even pressure.*

4 *An oval can be cut in a similar manner, using a template.*

5 *Cutting around a template requires practice as it is difficult to maneuver the cutter at the narrow ends of the oval.*

2

3

4

5

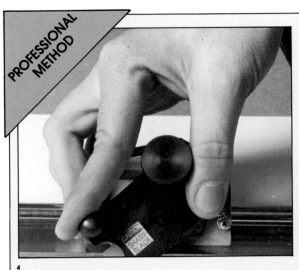

Cutting a beveled window
First the size of the border is determined; the depth of the bottom border is always greater than the depth of the other three, which are usually the same size. Once this is done, the total outside measurement of the window mat is calculated.
1 *Placing the mat card face down and using the straight edge of the mat cutter, the first side of the mat is cut.*
2 *The other three sides are then cut in the same way, altering the stops as appropriate.*

3 *The inner edges are then cut, using the beveled edge of the mat cutter. A slight overcut is usually made, as this will not show on the right side of the mat and results in the formation of sharp, clean, beveled corners.*

Some framers recommend using the beveled edge of the straight-edge to give the hand additional guidance although, since it is the hand itself that maintains the angle, this method still requires practice.

APPLYING LINES AND WASHES

To decorate the mat, lines can be drawn around the window and some of these filled in with washes. For an especially rich look, strips of gold are also applied. The number of lines, their thickness and spacing are important if you wish to avoid an over-fussy appearance and it is advisable to lightly pencil the lines around the window before applying the wash, measuring up in order to keep them strictly parallel.

A typical line-wash mat consists of a ruled line ¼ inch to ½ inch from the bevel, followed by a broader band of wash and enclosed by an outer double line. Ideally, the color of the wash and lines should echo some of the colors in the picture without swamping the image. Generally, bright colors should be avoided because they detract attention from the picture. If you particularly wish to use a strong color, such as viridian or magenta, try muting them slightly, without drastically changing them, by mixing a tiny amount of a complementary color with them. Black may seem an obvious choice for the lines but, on the whole, is better avoided, as the starkness of black dominates a light-colored mat too much and dark browns, greens or blues are preferable.

Before applying the wash, it is a good idea to wet the area between the lines, lightly wiping it with a soft watercolor brush dipped in water. The color will then flow onto the paper without leaving unsightly tide marks. Apply the color in several thin layers, until you achieve the required color density for your mat.

When the wash is completely dry, define the colored area with a stronger outline, using a ruling pen; usually the line is drawn in a deeper tone of the wash color. Wait until this line is completely dry before adding any other border lines, otherwise you may cause smudges with your hands, spoiling hours of painstaking work.

Lines
Before applying lines and washes, mark off all the measurements from the window outward (left). Mark these guidelines in light pencil all the way round the mat, or mark dots at the corners, or make pin holes if the line is to be particularly fine. Lines can be drawn with ruling pens, rapidographs, felt-nibbed pens, pencils or even crayons. A combination of different thicknesses and textures is usually more interesting than a regular arrangement.

Using a ruling pen
A ruling pen has an adjustable nib, allowing you to alter the thickness of the line. The pen can be filled by dipping it into the ink (below), but if you do this you must clean the edges afterward. Alternatively, load a brush with ink and fill the nib from this. Draw a line against a ruler (right), making sure that the ruler is upside down so that its beveled edge (bottom) creates a space, preventing the ink from touching the ruler directly.

Washes
Use pencil lines to guide you when applying lines and washes to mats. As a guide for the washes or to the finished lines themselves, draw lightly with a pencil against an ordinary clear ruler (right) You can then apply gouache freehand with a brush (below). Make sure the gouache is thin but creamy enough to be opaque.

Wash and line
All these washes and lines can be done by the home framer (left to right): silver and light gray on a dark background; sepia lines and a pale wash on white; black line and wash on medium; black, gold and white on light; compact white and dark on medium.

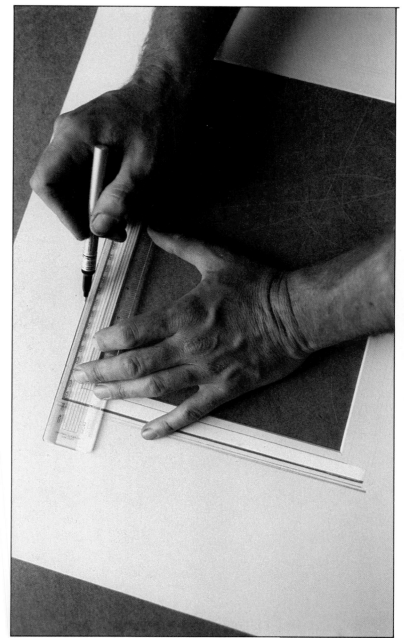

Types of line
Apply a line to a mat, using a gold pen (right). Lines can be drawn along the edges of a strip of wash to tidy it up, or they can be drawn first and a wash applied between them with a brush. They can also stand alone, in varying widths, if desired.

Wavy lines
Sometimes a wavy or irregular line can look attractive amid all the straight verticals and horizontals of the frame, the picture and the mount (above). Another attraction of wobbly lines is that they are easier to create than perfectly straight ones!

Use the beveled edge of a ruler to draw lines: place the ruler upside down on the mat, leaving a tiny gap between the paper and its raised edge so that the ink or paint will not blot should the color come into contact with the edge of the ruler.

Ordinary dip pens can be used to draw the lines but they are not very reliable, and by far the best way to achieve a continuous straight line is to use a ruling pen. Turn the knob on the side of the nib to adjust the width of the line but remember that the nib holds a limited amount of ink, so that a very wide line must necessarily be a very short one, as the color will run out very quickly; it is difficult to continue a broken-off line in a smooth fashion.

Gold and silver inks are more difficult to use than ordinary inks or watercolors: they are not so evenly mixed and can form sediments, making it harder to achieve a smooth flow. It is often a better idea to buy metallic adhesive strips, which can be cut to the required width. However, some of these are rather bright and care should be taken not to overdo the banding or the effect will be too brash.

COVERING THE MAT

Once the window has been cut, the mat can be covered with fabric. This is generally a better idea for oil paintings and heavier works than for watercolors.

The easiest method of covering a mat is to cut a piece of cloth slightly larger than the whole mat: glue this to the mat and then cut a window from it in such a way that flaps can be folded over to complete the covering. This method can be used with any shaped window, including round and oval ones. Use a spray adhesive for sticking the fabric to the mat.

CALCULATING THE LENGTH OF THE MOLDING

To work out the exact total length of molding that will be required, first add together the length and width of your picture and mat, if there is one, using the rabbet measurements (see page 56) and multiply the total by two. Next, to take account of the

Fabric-covered mats
When cutting fabric to cover a rectangular mat, allow enough material to fold over the edges. Cut slots into the inside and outside corners (right), so that they will fold back neatly. Place the fabric face down on a clean surface and spray on adhesive.

To discover the total length of molding you will require, measure the length and width of your artpiece, multiply the total by two and add ¹/₂ inch for an easy fitting margin. Multiply the width of the

molding by eight to allow for the mitered ends and add the result to the first figure.

molding that will extend beyond the picture at the corners of the frame, measure the width of the molding you have chosen and multiply this figure by eight. Add this to the first (picture) figure. This gives you the total length of molding needed.

CUTTING THE MOLDING

When cutting framers' molding into separate pieces it is important to avoid confusion by working always from the back edge, ie from the edge of the strip which contains the rabbet, and from the same end of the strip. It is also important to make one side of the frame at a time rather than trying to measure up the whole strip for cutting.

Cutting a Miter

Once you have determined the entire length of the molding that you require to frame your artpiece, your first task is to cut a miter at the end of the strip.

Cut small slots into the inside edge of an oval mat (above), so that they can be folded back in a curve.

Cutting a miter
1 *Place a piece of molding face up in a miter box to make the first cut. The rabbet edge of the molding fits up against the inside edge of the miter box.*

2 *If you are using a metal miter box, it can also be used as a corner clamp in the later gluing and nailing stage.*

Picture height | 2 × width of molding | Easy fitting margin

3 *Place the molding face up and measure it from the longest edge of the miter.*

4 *Mark the outside edge of the frame with a pencil. Line up the pencil mark with the cutting channel of the miter box and saw, making sure that the saw cut is on the waste side of the molding.*

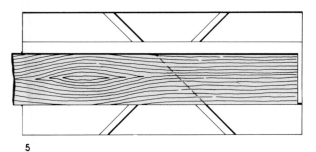

5 *Place the remaining piece of molding in the miter box and cut the first miter of the second strip.*

6 *Measure off the length of the second piece. Use the first piece as a guide, placing them back to back.*

A miter is the joint of two pieces of wood at an angle of 90 degrees, with the line of the junction exactly bisecting this angle. Precision is vital when cutting a miter: if the angle on one of the pieces is even slightly off 45 degrees, you will finish with a gap at the corners of the frame where the two pieces of molding should meet exactly. It is important to rule out the possibility of cutting a miter by simply measuring the angle and cutting the molding freehand. You would have to be extremely lucky to succeed in cutting a perfect miter using this method. A miter box or a miter cutter is essential for cutting perfect miters.

Place one end of the molding in the miter box, making sure that the back of the molding is absolutely flat on the bottom, the rabbet edge is nearest to you, and the strip is flush with the sides of the box. If you are using a metal miter box, place a thin strip of wood between the molding and the edge of the box, so that the metal does not mark the wood. If

you are using a metal miter box and a saw is not built into it, use a backsaw with it: the manufacturers will recommend the most suitable one. A wooden miter box is less expensive than a metal one and is used with a backsaw, preferably one with a thin blade. The miter box will guide the action of your saw precisely. Use a slow, easy cutting motion rather than a fast energetic one, which will cause the saw to turn and twist.

Now mark out the first total measurement — picture height plus twice the width of the molding plus easy-fitting margin — starting from the mitered end. There is no need to mark any other measurements on the strip at this point as the second strip will be cut based on the first length. Remove the molding from the miter cutter and lay it down with the rabbet upward. Mark the measurement on the outside edge of the molding. Then replace the molding in the miter cutter, with the mark in line with the channel of the cutter. This means that the mark is directly

1

3

2

Using a metal miter box
1 *This metal miter box has holes in its base so that is is not restricted to cutting angles of 45 degrees. Place pieces of dowling in the holes to allow you to change the angles for frames of more complex shapes.*
2 *Whatever type of miter box you use, always clamp it firmly to the work-table. Here, the framer has chosen to use a C-clamp.*
3 *Hold the molding firmly*

in position with one hand. The metal guides keep the sawing at a precise angle to ensure a perfectly fitting corner.

The Marples miter box
A popular model, the Marples miter box is a simple tool, which can be used as a corner clamp as well as a miter cutter.
1 *Hold the box in position on the work-table with a C-clamp.*
2 *Insert the wood into one of its sections and tighten the screws to hold it in place while the miter is cut.*
3 *Place the backsaw into its guides, holding it firmly.*
4 *Use a good quality saw and keep the sawing action steady for a clean cut.*

1

2

3

4

Variety of angles
1 *This more complicated miter box has a protractor fitted to it, which allows the user to cut a wide variety of angles to create triangles or otherwise-shaped frames.*
2 *It contains its own saw.*
3 *Set the saw carefully at the appropriate angle.*
4 *Hold the wood firmly in place against the metal support.*
5 *You will then be able to make an accurate cut with the saw.*
This miter box, like the others, is clamped to the work-bench by C-clamps. Make sure that it is securely held before setting angles and making cuts.

1

2

3

4

5

beneath the saw blade which will cut diagonally through the point to produce your second miter. You now have the first complete side of your frame.

You will now find that the remaining piece of molding already has a diagonal cut at one end, left over from the cut which created your first complete side. However, this is obviously facing the wrong way and, as an initial step to your second complete side, it is once again necessary to cut a first miter, from this same end. Next, place the complete side back to back with the remainder of the strip, putting the miter cuts together so that they are completely flush. Now to mark a diagonal line across the uncut strip, using the end of the first side as a guide. Place the uncut strip in the miter cutter and cut along the marked line to produce a second identical side for your frame.

Repeat this procedure for the other two sides of the frame, substituting the picture width measurement for the picture height measurement.

FORMING THE CORNERS

When joining two pieces of molding, first place them back to back to ensure that they are exactly the same length.

Using a Vice

Place one piece of molding in the vice and, if you are right-handed, hold the other piece in your left hand, keeping your right hand free to work with. Apply woodworkers' resin adhesive to the sawn-off mitered end of the length of molding held in the vice and hold the mitered end of the other piece firmly against it. Using an electric drill with a $\frac{1}{16}$ inch drill bit, make two pilot holes across the join, always ensuring that the drill passes right through into the

PROFESSIONAL METHODS

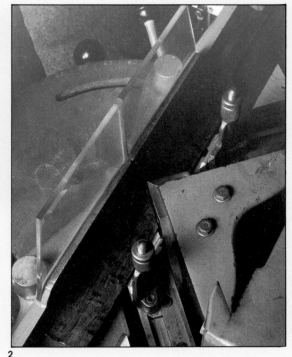

Cutting a wooden frame
1 *The strip of wooden molding is placed in the miter cutter, face up, with the outside edge toward the operator. Supports are wedged under the rabbet so that the descending blades do not crush it. The extra amount of molding required to accommodate the mitered ends is then calculated and allowed for and the machine operated.*
2 *The blades descend on the molding to cut out a triangle of wood. The cutter is then released. The cutter is worked several more times, each time cutting a little deeper. By cutting through the wood gradually in this way, the molding is not crushed and two perfect miters are created. The first length of the frame is then removed from the cutter and the rest of the strip moved along so that the next miters can be cut and the second length of frame completed.*

Cutting an aluminum frame
The strip of metal framing is placed in the metal miter cutter, with the outside edge facing the operator. The machine allows for the extra length needed to accommodate the mitered ends. The blades slice through the framing, leaving two precise miters.

second piece of wood; it is vital to hold the pieces firmly together so that there is no slipping as you drill. Now drive size 18 brads, ¾ inch long, into the pilot holes and release the left-hand piece of wood, which is now fixed to the molding held in the vice. To achieve a neat finish, countersink the brads, using a nail punch to drive them slightly below the surface, so that the hole can be filled with plastic wood filler.

If you do not have a drill, it is best to leave the glue to harden in the join before making a hole with a bradawl and nailing the pieces together. Modern rapid-dry glues set in half an hour to an hour.

Using a Clamp

If you have a miter clamp, sometimes called a corner clamp, instead of a vice, the task is made slightly easier, as the clamp holds both pieces together at rigid right angles, leaving both hands free to insert the brads after gluing.

Glues for Framing

Type	Advantages	Disadvantages	Drying times
Organic glue available in flakes or sheets	Set glue can be heated to dissolve, making it possible to correct mistakes	Time consuming and brittle; not as strong as PVA	Overnight
PVA	Convenient; no heat needed; very strong	Cannot break and re-set	Half an hour to overnight (depending on use and type)
Epoxy resins (there are several of these including the 'super glues')	Set quickly; very strong	Cannot break and re-set; spills and drips cannot be removed once set	A few minutes to an hour

1

3

Cramping methods
1 As an alternative to using corner clamps, a vice can be used, as long as it can accommodate two pieces of wood. Glue the mitered ends and place the two pieces together. Then make holes for nailing with a bradawl.
2 Another method of clamping is to use a clamp that consists of four metal corners, one of which has a screw attached. Run wire around the notches in the corners and tighten with the screw.
3 With the frame held firmly in place while the glue is drying, drill holes for the nails.

1

2

3

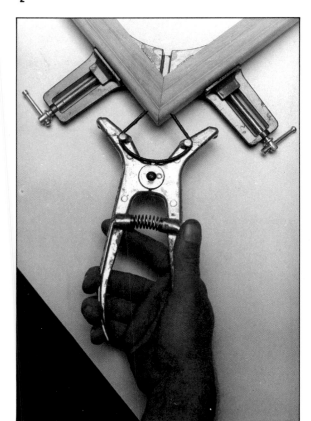

4

Corner clamps
1 *For lighter frames, corner clamps are useful. Fit the first piece of mitered wood into one side of the clamp.*
2 *Glue the second piece and place it into the clamp.*
3 *Ease the pieces together, making sure they are flush. Then tighten the clamp and wipe off any surplus glue.*
4 *If you are making a deep box frame, you may find that the clamps hold*
the bottom firmly but do not apply sufficient pressure to the top. In this case, position metal spring clips on the corner with pliers that first hold them apart and then release them onto the corner.

Checking corners
Lightweight clamps do not automatically make a precise right angle. Make the two 'L-shapes.' Then check the corner of the first two pieces (above) before fixing them
together to form a rectangle.

PROFESSIONAL METHOD

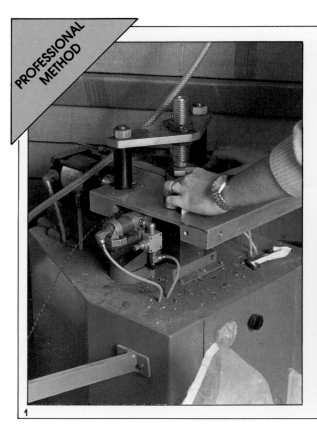

Underpinning
1 *The mitered ends of two sides of the frame to be joined are glued together and then placed face up in the underpinner. The machine is operated and a staple is forced up into the wood across the join.*
2 *The underpinner is worked several times along the join to ensure that the corner of the frame is made secure.*

CREATING A RABBET

Framers' molding comes with a fitted rabbet but if you buy builders' molding you will need to make your own rabbet — the 'step' beneath the frame itself into which the picture fits.

There are two basic ways of creating a rabbet. One method is to fix a wooden strip onto the molding before you begin cutting the miters. This piece of wood is called a quadrant and comes in a variety of sizes and woods. The other method is to make, in effect, two frames and then fit them together: the broader, top rectangle is the frame itself; the narrower one fits at the back to form the rabbet.

Using a quadrant

Select a strip of builders' molding and fix a rabbet strip to the back of this before you begin measuring the specific lengths and mitering the ends. Glue one side of the rabbet strip. Lay it flush with the outside edge of the molding and fix it from the back of the rabbet edge with brads. You have now made your own framers' molding and are ready to measure it and cut the miters in the usual way.

Making two frames

Begin by cutting the two shorter rabbet strips: measure the width of the artwork and add 1/8 inch to allow for easy fitting. This margin is particularly important when you frame canvases, as they are often a shade off-square and their corners are frequently bulky. Next cut the two longer strips: mea-sure the length of the artwork and add 1/8 inch plus twice the width of the strip. This method will allow the shorter strips to be fitted inside the longer ones. You do not need to cut miters on these rabbet strips as the rabbet will be stuck behind the frame and therefore does not need neat cornering.

Now cut the strips of molding for the outer frame. The ends of these strips must be mitered *(see pages 70–75)*. When cutting the top rectangle, remember that its final outer boundary — the measurement of all its outside edges — should be exactly the same length as the outer boundary of the rabbet rectangle so that when the two rectangles are fitted together, their outside edges will be flush with each other. The outer frame must overlap the inner edges of the rabbet rectangle to form the 'step' into which the picture will fit.

Next fit the pieces together, starting with the rabbet pieces. Apply glue evenly over the whole cut surface of the end of one of the shorter pieces. Then hold the glued end against the end of the inner side of one of the longer rabbet strips using a corner clamp or a vice to help the adhesive form a strong bond. Tap two brads into the end of the join to give extra stability. Repeat this process on all the corners, working in such a way that you produce two L-shapes, and finally join them both together to make the inner rectangle. Follow the same proce-dure with the mitered strips of wood to form the outer rectangle of the frame.

When the glue is dry, stick the two rectangles

Making a rabbet
Rabbets can be cut into pieces of molding with a rabbet plane (right). It is fitted with a steel depth gauge and an adjustable 'fence,' which can be set to the width of the rabbet required. Alternatively, stick a wooden strip, or quarter round, (below) along the length of a piece of molding.

Covering an insert
When making an insert, make sure you completely cover the front and the rabbet with fabric, so that *no bare wood will show when it is fitted into the main frame (above).*

together. Lay the rabbet rectangle flat and cover the whole of its top surface with adhesive. Place the outer rectangle face down and place the rabbeted rectangle adhesive-side down on top of the outer one. Fix it in position with brads. Make sure that the surface on which you are working is absolutely clean to avoid marking the front of the frame.

COVERING A FRAME INSERT
Strips of fabric are usually sufficient to cover wooden inserts. As inserts are made from strips of molding which then fit inside the outer frame, it is possible to cover the separate strips of insert molding before joining them together. If you do follow this method, the corners of the insert will be neat because the fabric will be glued between the joins.

Alternatively, you can cover the insert after it is assembled. Glue on strips of cloth and then miter the corners with a very sharp blade. The advantage of covering after assembly is that you avoid the difficulty of keeping the fabric clean while assembling the frame insert.

GLAZING
When your frame is completed, you may well wish to place the artwork beneath glass. For many frames, the procedure for cutting glass can be satisfactorily carried out at home, although any work involving glass must be completed extremely carefully.

Cutting very large pieces of glass, however, is best left to the expert: large pieces are difficult to carry; a

1

3

2

Cutting glass

1 There are two basic types of glass cutter. The most common type has a small tungsten carbide wheel. The other, a diamond glass cutter, is used mainly for thicker glass.
2 Use a ruler and felt-tipped pen to mark where you are going to cut the glass.
3 Keep the glass cutter lubricated by dipping it into special glass-cutting oil, a thin mixture, or methyl hydrate.
4 To score a line, hold the ruler firmly in place and keep the glass cutter vertical. This requires practice: too little pressure makes no impression at all and too much cracks the glass.
5 Tap the glass along the scored line with the knob on the end of the cutter.
6 Make the final snap by breaking the glass over the edge of a table.
7 If you are cutting a small section you can break it with glass pliers by placing the scored line along a table edge and giving the glass a sharp tweak.
8 Alternatively, break the glass by placing the scored line over the edge of a ruler.

suitable surface may be hard to find for a large operation; and the bigger the frame the greater the chance that your rabbet will be inaccurate.

The glass must fit very tightly inside the frame — it should not slip around inside the rabbet. Moreover, if the glass is a shade too big when cut, there is little you can do to rectify matters, although, occasionally, it may be possible to sandpaper it down to size. Measuring and cutting must, therefore, be very accurate and the allowance for easier fitting should ideally be no more than $1/20$ inch.

To enable you to avoid accidents with fragile picture glass it is advisable to practice glass cutting. Repeatedly cutting waste pieces of glass will increase your confidence and accuracy and it will also give you a good idea of the correct pressure that should be applied when cutting.

The surface on which you cut the glass should be completely level and non-slip. Use double-sided tape to prevent the glass and your straight-edge from moving.

Measure and mark the glass, preferably with a felt-tipped pen so that any wrong marks can be rubbed out with paint thinners if necessary. (Although, if you do leave any measurement marks, they are likely to be covered up in the last instance because the edges of the glass will be fitted under the rabbet.)

The next stage is the actual cutting: the object is not to cut through the glass completely but to score it, so that is can be snapped cleanly along the line. Place the straight-edge along the felt-tip mark and pull the cutter toward you with a pressure that is firm but not so firm that it cuts right through the glass. The scored line should pass cleanly over the edges of the sheet. Score the glass once only; twice makes little difference and can damage the cutting wheel even if you are using a tungsten carbide

4

5

6

7

8

wheel, which is superior to and much longer-lasting than an ordinary steel wheel.

There are several ways of snapping the glass. Most glass cutters have knobs on the end, which allow you to tap the glass along the cut: tapping gently but frequently ensures a clean snap. Another method of snapping is to slide the straight-edge beneath the glass, almost up to the score line but just to the immediate left of it. Then, when you press down on the right-hand side, the glass will snap, leaving a clean edge. Another method is to lift the glass slightly with your left hand (if you are right-handed), placing your thumb and first finger, with thumb on top, over the edge of the glass just to the left of the score line. Then take hold of the glass with your right hand just to the right of the score line. With one quick downward movement of your right hand the glass will snap.

Finishing, if required, can now be carried out by rubbing the edge of the glass with wet emery paper.

Remember that throughout the whole operation it is necessary to keep the glass cutter lubricated by frequently dipping it in paint thinners.

ASSEMBLING
Always work from the back of the frame and make sure that the surface on which you are working is clean. First insert the glass into the rabbet, making sure there is no dirt on it. Then insert the picture and

Assembling the frame
When assembling all the components, remember to work from the back (above). With the frame held face down, fit the glass into the rabbet at the rear. Then fit the matted picture, followed by the backing board, if this is being used. The oil painting and frame (right) are ready for assembly. Bradawl, steel tacks and hammer are necessary to secure the painting.

Using tacks
Ordinary steel tacks can be used to hold the components in place. After the frame has been assembled, tap the tacks into the inside edges of the main frame (left). One on each side should be enough to hold the frame together.

Using a point-driver
An alternative way of securing the components is to use a point-driver (above). Holding the machine down firmly onto the back of the assembled parts, pull the trigger to send a diamond tack into the inside edge of the main frame.

Gummed paper
To prevent dust from entering the framed picture, stick brown paper tape onto the back of the frame. Wet the paper first (above), and then stick it firmly along the back edges (right), making sure that the picture is completely sealed.

Strengthening corners
If the frame is heavy, it is advisable to strengthen it with corner pieces (above). These can be home-made triangles of hardboard. Glue and then tack them into place on the back corners of the frame. Make sure that they are placed so that they are not visible from the front.

Fastening to the wall
Some frames, especially deep ones, look good when screwed up flat against the wall. Fastening plates can be bought for this (right). For hanging most framed pictures, screw-eyes and wire are ideal (below right).

mat, if there is one, face down on the glass. Finally, insert the backing board. There are several ways of holding everything in place. If the rabbet is deeper than the thickness of all the parts, hammer brads into the rabbet, behind the backing board, at intervals of 2 inches. If the parts are thicker than the rabbet, hammer the brads into the back of the frame and bend the heads over the backing board. If the backing board lies flush with the back of the frame, it is a good idea to hold everything in place with turn clips. Once everything is assembled, seal the edges with strips of brown paper tape. This prevents any dust from entering.

HANGING
Using a bradawl, punch a hole either side of the frame about a third of the way down. Screw in screw eyes. Then run picture-framing wire through the eyes, knotting it at either end with pliers. Take care not to leave the wire too taut. Finally, wind the spare ends back round the wire.

PROFESSIONAL METHOD

1

2

3

Assembling an aluminum frame

1 Chevrons are placed on either end of the top strip of the frame and screwed into place from the back. The two adjoining strips are then inserted into the chevrons and also screwed into place. The picture, backing and glass are then slid into the frame and the final side of the frame screwed into place.

2 Springs are inserted between the backing board and the back of the frame toward the corners to keep the picture pressed against the glass.

3 Two butterfly clips are inserted into the frame a third of the way down each side of the picture. These are then turned and knocked firmly into place. Wire is then threaded through one butterfly clip and twisted round on itself. Any extra wire is clipped off with a wire cutter. The wire is threaded through the other clip in the same way and the picture is ready for hanging.

Finishing techniques

Finishing the frame provides an ideal opportunity for experiment. You can transform the bare appearance of builders' molding in a wide variety of ways by choosing any of the following basic finishing techniques and adapting them to your own personal taste. Remember to bear in mind the type of artpiece you are framing when deciding on the finish.

APPLYING GESSO

To create a perfect finish, it is advisable to treat the wood surface with gesso before painting or gilding it. This prevents paint or size from sinking into it and also provides a fine, smooth surface on which to apply the final touches.

Gesso is a fine white powder, rather like plaster of Paris, and is available from art stores (full instructions are provided with the product). Work the white gesso powder into rabbit-skin glue to a thin, milk-like consistency; brush onto the surface and allow to dry. Apply a second coat and, when it is dry, lightly rub it down to achieve a completely smooth finish.

GILDING WITH REAL GOLD LEAF

Gilding is the technique of placing a fine film of gold over a surface. Real gold leaf comes in the form of 'leaves' in a booklet and covers a gesso-treated surface best. Gold leaf is so fine that its final color can be affected by the color of the surface beneath it. Traditionally, therefore, before applying the gold leaf, the gesso base is given a coat of red bole, a red clay pigment that gives a rich, warm look to the gold finish.

There are two main methods of gilding with real gold leaf: water gilding and oil gilding.

Water Gilding

Used to achieve a high-gloss finish, ideally, you should be taught this method by a professional and even then a great deal of practice is needed to attain perfection. However, it is still a fruitful field for experiment by the more determined home framer.

Gesso and bole are applied to the wooden frame, which is then coated with water, and, finally, gold leaf. The leaf is then burnished to achieve the

Rabbit skin glue
Gesso can be bought ready-made, but if you want to make your own you must first bind the gesso powder by mixing it with rabbit skin glue. The glue is bought in granules or sheets and should be soaked in water overnight. Mix one part soaked glue to nine parts cold water, and gently heat the mixture in a double boiler. Add the gesso powder, usually referred to as gilders' whiting, until it has a creamy white consistency. Sieve out any lumps or strain through muslin.

1

3

2

Applying gesso
1 First seal the wooden frame with a weak solution of rabbit skin glue and water.
2 Apply the first coat of gesso.
3 As soon as this has dried, rub it down with fine sandpaper, or wet and dry. To build up a smooth gesso base, repeat this procedure up to six times.

Building up gesso

1 When the final coat of gesso has dried, rub it down to an extremely fine finish with wet and dry. At this stage you can actually wet the wet and dry. (Had you tried this at an earlier stage it would have dissolved the gesso and taken you back to the bare wood.)

2 Use a sculpting tool to remove excess build up of gesso in the corners of the frame.

3 The gesso coat should be perfectly smooth before adding the final finish.

1

2

3

Applying bole

Before gilding, apply two or three coats of bole (left). Apply the first coat very thinly (below). Allow each coat to dry before rubbing down with fine sandpaper.

classic shine associated with gilded frames.

First apply the coats of hard gloss, that is, gesso that has been mixed with a large amount of glue to a hard consistency: two coats of hard gesso are usually sufficient. Then apply up to four coats of soft gesso, and sandpaper them finely. Now apply up to four coats of bole and rub down the surface with fine sandpaper to achieve an absolutely smooth finish. With a soft mop brush apply water containing a small amount of gelatine or methyl hydrate and then place the gold leaf in position straight away. Finally, burnish the leaf, using a gilders' burnisher. If the burnisher cannot reach the small indentations in the more intricately molded or carved frames, leave them mat; this adds to the richness of the finish by producing a variety of tone.

Oil Gilding

For oil gilding: there is no need to apply the first coats of hard gesso and you can brush an ordinary coat of paint instead of the bole directly onto the gesso, ignoring the color aspect altogether.

Oil gilding requires a non-absorbent surface and a coating of shellac glue is required to completely seal the surface. If you do not wish to use bole but do wish to achieve something of the earth-red color which is such a good base for gold leaf, red colorant can be added to the shellac glue before it is applied. Ordinary red oil paint can also be used in this way. For silver leaf, black or yellow ocher are good colors to use for the base instead of red.

The surface must be slightly sticky before applying the sheets of gold leaf. This is achieved by coating the surface with gold size, a mixture of oil varnish and a drying agent, designed to provide exactly the right degree of 'tackiness.' Gold size is readily obtainable from picture framers' supply stores.

SIMPLE GILDING

The alternatives to real gold leaf do not provide such an effective gilded finish but they are less expensive and simpler to apply.

Transfer Gold Leaf

All that is needed prior to positioning the transfer is to give the gessoed frame a coat of thin Venetian red acrylic paint. Then simply lay the transfer gold leaf on the surface and rub over it firmly with your fingers before stripping off the backing.

Metallic Powders

Apply straight onto the tacky surface; again a ground color is desirable to give a rich sheen. Metallic powders are not suitable for large areas as they tend to look thin and insubstantial. After applying a powder, a coat of varnish is necessary to prevent it from being rubbed off the surface.

Wax Gilding

Again, there is no need for either gesso or bole. Simply apply an undercoat of paint to the wooden frame. Then make your own 'gilt' by mixing wax with metallic powder and rub this over the completely dry painting frame. Polish with a soft rag.

Gold or Silver Paint

Paint cannot usually be used to create the impression of gilding, although it can be useful occasionally for touching up small areas of gilding.

Wax gilding
Mixed wax and metallic powder is applied with a brush over an orange undercoat (left). *It can also be applied with the finger* (below). *The proportion of wax to powder depends on the density of the metal finish required. Pre-mixed metallic wax is also available.*

Transfer gilding

Before applying transfer gilding, make sure that the surface has been coated with gold size. It is important that this has dried to the right degree of tackiness to ensure that the gold adheres properly to the surface. Different types have different setting times, so follow the manufacturers' instructions.

1 *Transfer gold comes in sheets on a paper backing.*

2 *Position a sheet on the frame.*

3,4 *Press it down lightly with the finger. Use a tool if you have to push it into a grooved molding.*

5 *Carefully remove the paper backing. Repeat this procedure until the required area is covered. Traditionally, red-brown bole is used as a base for gold, and black bole for silver. After applying the transfer gold, protect it with a coat of lacquer.*

1

2

4

3

5

Water gilding

You will need a gilders' pad and knife, a badger brush and a thin solution of rabbit skin glue and water.

1 *Cut the gold leaf on the pad with the knife to the required size. This requires practice, as the leaf is very flimsy and tends to waft in the slightest draft.*

2 *Create static on a badger brush by rubbing it gently on the skin or hair, and pick up the leaf with it.*

3 *Place the water solution carefully on the area to be gilded, and brush into place.*

4 *The framer has used red lacquer to complete the design.*

1

2

3

4

STAINING

Staining enhances rather than hides the natural patterns of the wood grain. Hardwoods take the stain particulary well, as their close-grained nature aids the even application of the dye. Softwoods are not so suitable for staining and should be well sanded beforehand.

Many colors of wood dye are available and they can be mixed to give further subtle shades. Stains used to be restricted to the more natural-looking colors but nowadays bright colors, too, are available.

Stains can be oil based or water based and care should be taken not to mix the two. Wood dye can be evenly spread with a soft brush, although it is often best to apply the dye with very fine steel wool, using rubber gloves to protect your hands. It is often easier to dye the separate pieces of molding before assembling the frame. Rub the wood with turpentine before staining to remove any oil or grease marks.

WAXING

Natural or stained wood should be sealed to preserve its color. The most natural-looking method of achieving this is to use wax. After the wood has been lightly rubbed down with a fine sandpaper, apply white polish, beeswax or ordinary household wax polish. Then buff the wax to give a sheen.

VARNISHING

A varnish provides a tough, hard-wearing finish but never gives quite the same professional look as wax

Antiquing silver transfer leaf
A silver transfer leaf frame can be antiqued with black staining wax—the type used on furniture. Rub it in with a rag, wait a few minutes, and then buff it up lightly to achieve a polished finish.

The same treatment can be used effectively on other finishes, including watercolor or gouache.

or polish. Varnishes are available in high-gloss, mat or semi-gloss; the high-gloss varnishes, however, can look shiny and synthetic and are probably best suited to bright and modern subjects.

ANTIQUE GLAZING

One way to give a frame an older look is to coat the frame with a subdued colored glaze. This can be done over a plain color or over a decorative painted effect.

Antique glaze can be purchased ready-made but it is simple to make: just add linseed oil, turpentine or paint thinners and a drying agent to the oil color chosen. Artists' oil paints provide a wide choice of colors, and earth pigments, such as raw or burnt umber or raw sienna, are popular because of their natural mature look but if you are antiquing a metal surface, plain black functions well as the basic glaze color.

When you have mixed the glaze, apply it evenly over the frame: the brush should follow the direction of the wood grain. Then wipe off the glaze with a cloth, taking care not to wipe it away completely but to leave traces in the cracks and corners. This can be made permanent by giving the frame a coat of varnish when it is dry.

Oil-based glazes take a long time to dry, possibly a few days. Water-based tinted washes dry more quickly and can be made easily: tint very thin latex paint with watercolor or acrylic paint.

ANTIQUE SPATTERING

Antique spattering produces a freckled, mature look. The neutral colors that are used with glazes are best suited to this technique, although grays and black can also look attractive; use an antique glaze or Indian ink. Spattering can also be effective in toning down a too-bright underneath color.

Dip the stiff bristles of a brush into the glaze, paint or ink and spatter it unevenly over the frame by drawing your thumb over the top of the brush so that tiny spots of paint are flicked onto the surface. If the spatter is applied too evenly it looks like a mechanical paint finish, so make sure to keep the pattern random. If the finished effect looks rather stark, rub it down with a little steel wool when it is dry.

When the spattered frame is dry, add a coat of varnish to protect it. A high-gloss finish is not suitable for a frame that you wish to look old, so use mat or semi-gloss varnish.

APPLYING FLAT PAINTS

Acrylic paints give a quick-drying and convenient basic coat, which can be left plain or waxed, or can be varnished or embellished with oil- or water-based paints.

Acrylics allow you to begin with a gray or neutral tone to which you can add subtle shades of a brighter color to give a slightly warmer or cooler effect. To achieve this, mix a little of the color to the gray

Scumbling
Apply a flat, oil-based undercoat. Here light gray is being used with brown and blue mottling. You can work with bought scumble glaze or make your own from artists' oil paint, linseed oil and turpentine. Using the lightest glaze and a soft bristle brush, stipple the *surface in order to achieve an even but broken color (left). Then apply a darker tone of scumble with a smaller brush (below left), aiming for a linear, veined effect. The finished frame is shown beside a darker* *version made with a dark gray undercoat and a light scumble glaze (below right).*

acrylic base and apply it as one coat; or apply a coat of flat gray acrylic paint and, after it has dried, apply a top coat of very diluted paint so that the gray shows through a translucent layer of color.

Oil-based paints can also be used as finishes but take longer to dry. Modern high-gloss or 'wet-look' paints are more suited to a modern picture or frame. They are most effective as a finish when used with a light undercoat or gesso surface, which is lightly sanded. If gesso is not being used, coat the wood with wood primer before applying an oil-based paint.

Spray paints and enamels give a really professional-looking finish, free of any tell-tale brush marks around the mitered corners. They are particularly effective when applied to a surface that has been primed with gesso. They can be applied directly onto a well-sanded base of acrylic or latex paint but should not be used on an oil-based undercoat.

SCUMBLING

Best suited to plain, flat, angular frames, scumbling is a quicker way of achieving a marbling effect, although it does not have the same quality of finish. It consists of a flat undercoat, with more than one tone of scumble glaze on top applied with a circular motion of the brush. Mix scumble glaze from artists' oil paint, linseed oil and turpentine—to give it its 'glaze' or transparent quality. Alternatively, buy it ready-made in a variety of colors.

MARBLING

Like tortoiseshelling, marbling is done not to deceive the eye into thinking that it is seeing real marble but to produce a beautiful pattern based on the subtle markings of marble — it is a visual association rather than an exact replica. Again, it is a technique suited to plain, flat, angular frames rather than ornate moldings, on which it would be impossible to create this style.

Paint an all-over glaze, made from paint thinner and artists' oil paint, over the surface. Paint the veins of the marbling pattern onto this in short, jerky strokes, rolling and flicking the brush to give an impression of the actual seams in the stone. Before the veins are dry, blur them very thoroughly with a dry brush. Then go over it again, using the same colors and painting a few better defined veins onto the blurred background. This is surprisingly simple and effective and, providing that you use fairly neu-

1

2

3

Marbling

1 *Starting with a cream ground, apply a loose ocher glaze. Use a smaller brush to rough in veins of dark brown.*

2 *Ruffle and blend the wet surface with crumpled newspaper. Soften the surface with a dry brush.*

3 *With a small artists' brush, add veins in blue and sepia glaze. Soften these with a broad brush or a feather.*

4 *Apply unsoftened, fine white veins with the tip of the feather to cross the existing pattern.*

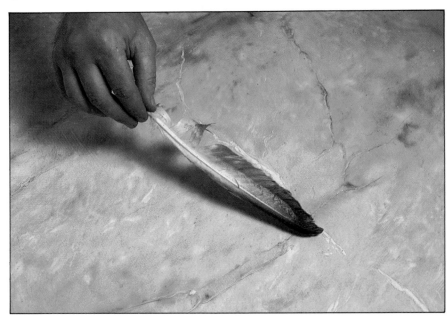

4

Types of marble

Terra verde or green marble (above left) is made by applying green and white glazes over a black base. White marble (center left) is created by painting thin black and gray veins over a white base. Golden marble (below left) is built up from ocher, sepia, blue and white glazes over cream.

Pattern and texture

1 The framer is applying his own mixture of wax and black stain with a cloth to create a pattern.

2 A motif has been etched into the gesso base and decorated with a water-based paint and gold wax.

3 This frame was made from a piece of flat timber, which was coated with gesso and decorated with gold leaf and blue lacquer.

4 In this frame, a dark blue lacquer and gold motifs were used in a similar way.

1

3

2

4

tral colors without too much tonal contrast, it will produce a fine marble effect that will not intrude too much upon the picture.

TEXTURING

A textured finish is best suited to simple frames. A texture can be scratched into a paint surface to soften the effects of an austere frame without detracting from its simplicity. The traditional craftsman's method is to scratch or carve out a pattern on a gesso ground. A more practical and quicker way is to use a vinyl paint as the base.

Apply a thick coat of vinyl paint to the frame and texture it when the paint is partially dry so that it will be stiff enough to hold its shape and preserve the patterns you make. A simple, linear texture effected with a metal comb, a stiff brush or any other sharp implement can make an intriguing textured surface, turning a commonplace frame into an unusual one. Once you have created the textured surface, paint it any color you wish.

WOOD-GRAINING

Wood-graining is a traditional technique, the object of which is not to produce a finish that looks exactly like wood but to produce a frank replica of a wood-grain pattern with paint. A coat of paint is applied, a glaze added and then wood-grain marks made on this. It is not necessary to confine

yourself to "woody" colors — some of the most exciting modern grain has been created in colors which were never seen in any natural habitat.

Start off by applying a coat of flat color. This should be lighter than the glaze and, ideally, there should not be too much contrast between the two as the effect will be too stark. Use ordinary undercoat, or mat or eggshell latex paint for the first coat; high gloss and enamel paints should not be used.

You can either buy the glaze and then tint it with a stainer — a strong, transparent liquid color — or you can make your own, using the same method as for making antiquing glaze but with any color. Brush a thin glaze of color over the dry, undercoated surface, using a small decorators' brush, about the size of one normally used to paint a window-frame.

While the glaze is still wet, drag a brush with slightly spaced bristles across the surface to create hair-like streaks. Now flick a special grainers' brush — a soft brush known as a "flogger" and available from specialist art stores — evenly over the surface to give a blurred effect.

TORTOISESHELLING

Tortoiseshelling gives a frame a luxurious finish, creating an unusual and special-looking effect. Care should be taken, however, not to overdo it because tortoiseshelling is essentially a paint finish

Wood-graining
There are two methods of wood-graining. In the first (right), medium oak scumble glaze is applied on top of a pale, wood-colored undercoat. Both are specially available for wood-graining. While the glaze is wet, it is combed with a rubber comb. The combed ridges are then smoothed out diagonally with a soft brush to create a softer line. In the second (far right, above), a paint glaze is brushed on freely and combed. Knots are touched in with a fingertip and then strengthened with an artists' brush. In the third method (far right, below), a soft dragger is used to create a mahogany pattern in wet, red-brown paint.

Golden tortoiseshell
1 *On a cream undercoat, apply tinted varnish in short, irregular strokes. Indian red blobs are also put on with a small decorators' brush.*
2 *Blend these in long, smooth strokes.*
3 *Apply blobs of Indian red and burnt sienna and work these in lightly with an artists' brush.*
4 *Blend these with a swift, crossing stroke. Finally, soften the whole surface by criss-crossing lightly with a wide, dry brush.*

1

2

3

4

— a frankly fake, exotic production, which can look overwhelming if it covers a very large area.

The tortoiseshell pattern is based on the polished pieces of tortoiseshell that show the internal seams of organic growth and feature them as a pattern. Originally, tortoiseshelling was applied mainly to small articles, such as combs, hairbrushes and dressing table mirrors, but it is now a popular paint finish for many surfaces, especially the surfaces of small items of furniture and picture frames. Study the style carefully and decide which of the varieties you require. They range from very dark to what is often referred to as blond tortoiseshell and the finished effect can be of blobs of spreading color or, alternatively, of streaks.

The darkest styles of tortoiseshelling include one which is very distinctive and rich-looking. It was used

a great deal on Colonial-style furniture and is usually recognizable by its bold, dark streaks — often black or bronze — running over a mellow red background. Blond tortoiseshelling is effected over a light-colored background, which may be metallic — using gold or silver. Fawn or light brown is usually used for the streaks.

Use a smooth, oil-based paint for the initial ground on which the pattern is to be based. The ground color should be of a lighter tone than that of the required finish because the varnish and streaks will darken it. The key to successful tortoiseshelling is to work the design into the varnish while it is still wet, spreading successive layers of paint into patterns by lightly brushing diagonally in opposite directions with a dry brush. Use oil-based paints, such as artists' oil colors, for the streaks.

The Practice of Framing

THE PROJECTS

1

2

3

4

5

6

7

8

MAN RAY

ROSE COTTAGE

99

PROJECT 1

Framing a poster

This is a simple project—a poster is clipped beneath a sheet of glass to an ordinary piece of particle board. However, deterioration will develop unless steps are taken to strengthen this heavy artpiece and to preserve the poster from damage due to contact with the particle board. To overcome these problems, a backing is provided for the poster and wooden strips are fixed to the edges of the particle board. Screw clips can then be fixed to the wooden strips rather than the particle board, which is not really suitable for this, making the artpiece more secure and, at the same time, giving a more professional look to the piece.

Materials and Equipment

Poster	Small brads
Wooden strip,	Cardboard
$^1/_4$ inch wide	Clips
Particle board	Bradawl
Ruler	Short screws,
Craft knife	$^3/_8$ inch long
Pencil	Cut and smoothed glass,
Backsaw	$^1/_2$ inch or
Miter box	$^1/_8$ inch thick
Hammer	Screwdriver
Resin glue	Screw-eyes or D-rings
Regular brads	Strong wire or cord

Glass

Backing

Poster

Wood strip

Particle board

1 Select a length of wooden strip, $^1/_4$ inch wide, and a piece of ordinary particle board. Measure the post to be framed and cut the particle board to the same size minus $^1/_2$ inch in both height and width to account for the width of the strip.

2 Cut each piece of wooden strip to a length which is $^1/_2$ inch longer than the corresponding side of particle board. Then, using a miter box, cut the corners of the frame in the strips. Using ordinary resin glue, fix the strips around the edges of the particle board and nail them together with brads.

3 Glue and nail a piece of wooden strip across the back of the particle board, using small, $^1/_2$ inch brads to avoid penetrating the front of the board. It is from this strip that the artpiece will be hung on the wall, so place it one third of the way down from the top of the particle board to hide the hanging-wire.

4 From cardboard, cut a piece of backing to the size as the poster. This will be placed between the poster and the particle board to prevent damage being caused to the poster by the rough texture of the particle board. The backing also lends a firmness to the final fitting and presents a smooth resting place for the poster.

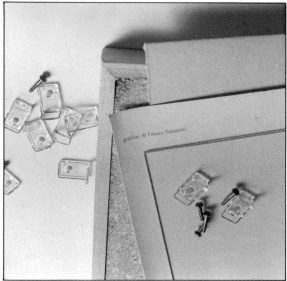

5 You are now ready to fix glass, poster, backing and particle board with clips. Sprung-steel emu clips are simple and popular but, for extra strength, a hardware or brass-fitting store can supply clips of the type shown here in brass, stainless steel, or the less noticeable acrylic, which we have chosen.

6 Position each clip carefully. Place two clips on the top, two on the bottom, and three on each side to hold the poster and glass securely. Make sure that the clips are a few inches away from the corners and are neatly opposite each other. Their positions can now be marked with a bradawl.

7 To make holes for the screws that will fix the clips, hold the bradawl firmly but do not push and twist too hard. Only small holes need be made, as the best type of screw for fixing clips is a short, $3/8$ inch one.

8 The component parts are now ready for assembling. Place the particle board on a flat surface. Lay the backing board on top, then the poster, and finally the glass. Purchase glass either $1/12$ inch or $1/8$ inch thick but avoid anything thicker. Ask the glazier to smooth off the edges, or smooth them yourself with fine sandpaper.

9 Screw the clips into the wooden strips round the edges of the particle board, using a small screwdriver. You will probably find it easiest to start the screws while the assembled poster and board are lying flat on the work-table. They can then be finished firmly, with the poster upright if necessary.

10 Lay the framed poster face down. Fasten two screw-eyes, or D-rings, onto the strip across the back of the particle board. To make hanging easier, keep these spaced wide apart. Run a strong wire or cord through each eye and fasten it so that it is fairly taut; knot it firmly. You may find it better to use the wire or cord doubled.

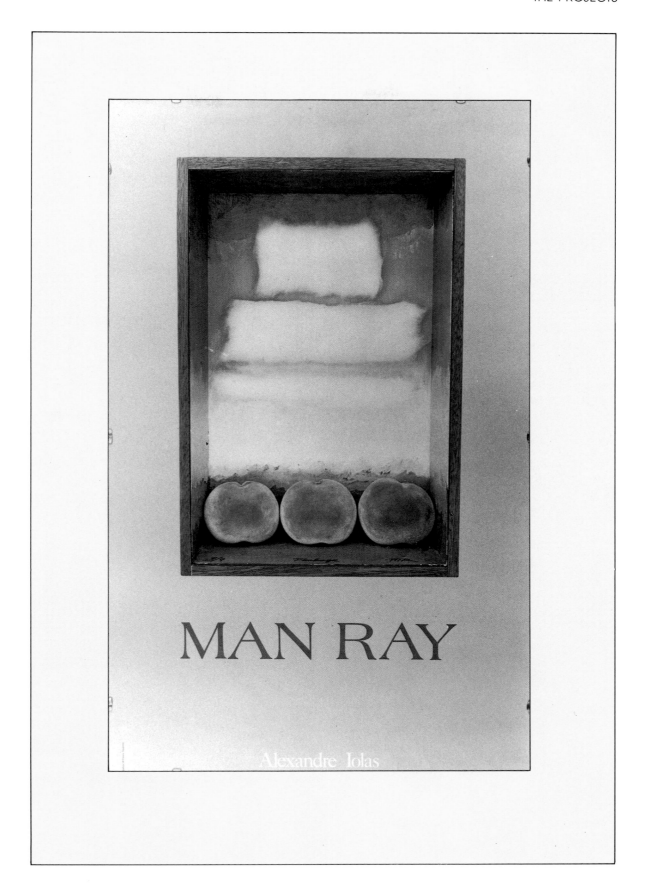

MAN RAY

Alexandre Iolas

PROJECT 2

Framing a watercolor

1 To frame this large watercolor, it was decided to use a deep, white mat, with two inner slip mats, in colors matching those in the painting.

The delicate lines and washes of a watercolor usually require a mat to set them off best. Moreover, watercolors are normally framed behind glass, which helps to preserve them, and the mat acts as a fixture to prevent the watercolor being pressed too tightly against the glass.

Materials and Equipment

Ruler
Hard, sharp pencil
Craft knife or scalpel
Thick, white mat card
Thin, colored mat
  card
Aluminum-plated
  wooden molding
Saw
Miter box
Woodwork glue
Heavy-duty cardboard
Glass, ¹/₁₂ inch thick

Point-driver (optional)
Nails
Hammer
Brown paper tape
Hardboard offcuts for
  corner pieces
Bradawl
Corner clamps
Screwdriver
Screw-eyes for wall-
  hanging
Brass picture-frame wire
Pliers

2 Measure with even more care than usual when making slip mats, as even a slight error is easily noticeable in a multi-mat. Slip mats are usually the same width all round, while the outside mat is deeper at the bottom than on the other three sides to ensure that the picture sits up well in the frame. Cut the mats and windows.

Glass

Frame

Mat

Watercolor

Backing
board

Inner slip
mat

Inner slip
mat

3 Measure the perimeter of the outer mat and cut a metal frame, mitering the corners in the usual way. You can obtain solid metal frames, which must be cut with a hacksaw, but the frame we chose was essentially wooden, with a coating of light aluminum, which enabled us to cut it with an ordinary saw. Glue the pieces together; do not nail the pieces in this case— nails would make the metal look untidy. Cut a piece of cardboard, measured to fit inside the frame, for the backing board.

4 Turn the frame over and fit the pre-cut glass into the rabbet. Next insert the triple mat, then the watercolor and finally the backing board. To hold this large frame together, a point-driver was used to tack the components together. Position the point-driver right up against the inside wooden part of the frame.

5 Holding the machine down firmly on the backing board, pull the trigger and shoot a diamond-tack into the side of the frame. If you do not have a point-driver, tack the nails sideways into the inside of the frame.

6 It will now be necessary to stick the brown paper tape to the edges of the backing board and the back of the frame to reinforce the structure and keep out the dust. Wet strips of ordinary brown paper tape.

7 Press the tape into place, working slowly and carefully to ensure that no possible space is left for dust to enter. Take extra care when pressing the tape into the corners.

8 Trim off any excess tape with a scalpel. The back of the frame should now be thoroughly sealed. This is very important, as watercolors can easily be spoiled by dust and dirt.

9 To strengthen the corner joins, which were not nailed, as this is a metal frame, we made corner pieces from hardboard. You can also buy ready-made corner pieces in a variety of metals, if you wish.

10 The corner pieces are first glued and then nailed into place. Run strips of glue along the edges of the corner pieces. Try not to use too much glue as this might cause slippage.

11 Place the corner pieces into position with extreme care; make sure they are not visible from the front of the frame. Glue into place, then wait for the glue to harden.

12 Using a bradawl, make holes in the back of the frame for nailing the corners. A steady hand pressure is essential to ensure that you do not damage the frame. Tap in the nails.

13 We used special brass picture-framing wire, obtainable from art shops, for this project, to bear the weight of the artpiece. Run the wire through one of the eyes and knot it. Tighten the knot with pliers and then wire and knot the other end, taking care not to leave the wire too taut. Wind the spare ends back around the wire.

14 A bradawl should be used to make holes in the back of the metal frame for hanging. Position the holes about a third of the way down the picture, one on either side, and screw in screw eyes.

15 The framing is now complete. Without dominating the picture, the slip mats lead the eye into the watercolor and enhance the pale washes that were used in the painting.

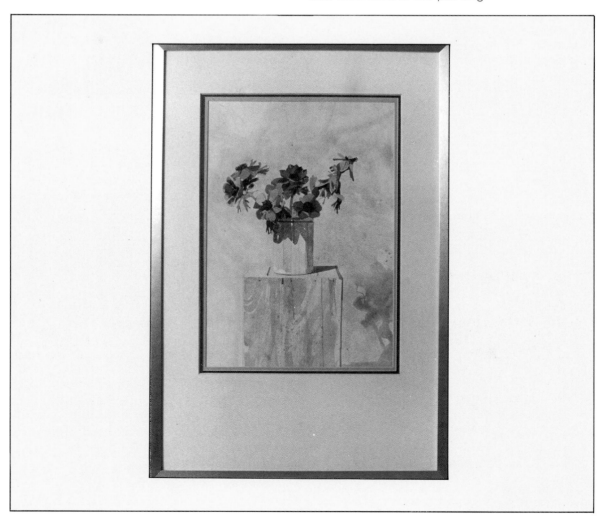

PROJECT 3

Framing an oil painting

T his modern, dramatic oil painting stares boldly from the canvas. The wintry image is flat and graphic, and we therefore decided to use a deep box frame, painted a stark plain black to highlight the dramatic nature of the picture. We decided not to place the painting under glass; it is generally not necessary to glaze oil paintings.

Materials and equipment

Pine molding, 2 inches by 1 inch	Tape
Hard, sharp pencil	Bradawl
Ruler	Punch
Saw	Fine surface filler
Miter box	Sandpaper
Woodwork glue	Gray undercoat paint
Corner clamps	Black enamel spray paint
Corner clips (optional)	Paintbrush
Pliers	Steel tacks
Nails	Brass plate wall-fastenings
Hammer	Brass screws
Wooden quarter round	Screwdriver

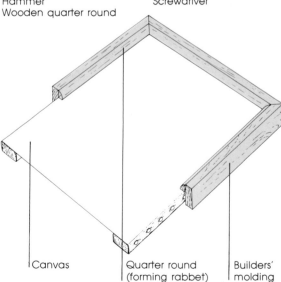

Canvas   Quarter round (forming rabbet)   Builders' molding

1 We chose pinewood, 2 inches by 1 inch, generally available from building suppliers, for the main frame. When measuring for oil painting frames, remember that the canvas on the stretcher is often slightly misshapen, so allow a tiny extra margin. After cutting and mitering, glue the corners and clamp them together.

2 This is a deep frame and the clamps are holding it firmly together at the bottom. However, there is no clamping pressure on the top and we used special sprung-steel clips to rectify this.

3 To fit the clips, special pliers are required to pull them apart. Position the pliers around the top of one corner, as shown, and release them, allowing the clip to spring into place.

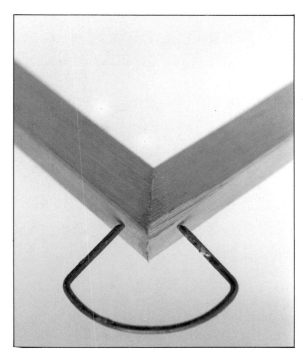

4 Fit clips similarly on each corner, so that the frame is firmly held by clamps and clips. If you do not have special clips, tie string round the frame as a temporary measure. Then tap in nails to secure the corners, using a punch to tap them just below the surface.

5 Allow the time specified by the manufacturer for the glue to dry, before releasing the clamps and clips.

6 The wooden frame should fit snugly around the canvas. A rabbet is now fitted to cover the edges of the canvas, giving a neater and more professional look and stopping the canvas from slipping out through the front. A wooden quarter round was chosen to make the rabbet. Miter the quarter round and place the strip onto the front of the frame, so that you can measure the lengths required. Mark off each corner and cut to size.

7 Glue the rabbet strips into place. Bind strips of tape around the quarter round and frame to hold it in place, and wait for the glue to set.

8 This solid, deep frame will stand upright without difficulty, and it is therefore easy to work holes into the quarter round and frame with a hand-held bradawl. Tap in the nails and sink them below the surface with a punch.

9 Fill in the nail holes with fine surface filler, obtainable from most hardware stores. At the same time fill in the holes made in the corners of the main frame. Then rub down the filler with sandpaper.

10 Brush a gray undercoat onto the completed frame, applying two coats. Sand this down. Then spray thinly with black enamel paint. Allow this to dry and then rub down gently with fine steel wool. Spray on several coats in this way, until you have achieved the finish you require.

11 The components are now ready for assembly. You will need a bradawl, hammer and steel tacks. Make sure that you have a flat, uncluttered surface on which to lay the frame for final fitting.

12 Fit the canvas into the main frame, easing it up tight against the rabbet. Check that it fits snugly before nailing. Then, using a hand-held bradawl, make the holes in the inside of the frame. Nail steel tacks sideways into the frame to hold the painting in place.

13 It was decided to fit the frame against the wall instead of hanging it and we selected brass plate fastenings for this, to be fitted to the sides of the frame. Position the plates so that they are exactly opposite each other and mark the holes with a bradawl. Screw on the plates with brass screws.

14 Screw the framed painting in place on the wall. It should sit flat against the wall to enhance the depth of the frame and give emphasis to the window effect of this landscape picture.

PROJECT 4

Framing a collection of photographs

All the people in the photographs to be framed are from the same family, and all the photographs have a definite nineteenth-century flavor. They are therefore ideal candidates for a group matting — all the photographs matted within one large frame. By using a single mat with several windows cut into it, a backing board and glass — held in the rabbet of a polished wooden frame that is enchanced by a gold slip — vitality and unity is given to what could easily be a collection of scattered photographs.

Materials and Equipment

Stiff card or hardboard	Miter box
Mat card	Saw
Sharp, hard pencil	Middle oak woodstain
Ruler with beveled edge	Rag
Protractor or try square	Woodwork glue
Craft knife	Clear wax
Brown paper tape	Gold slip
Clear ruler	Glass, $1/12$ inch thick
Brown sepia ink	Steel tacks, 1 inch long
Gold ink	Hammer
Lining pen or felt-tipped	Screwdriver
pen	Brass screw eyes
Rabbeted molding	Picture-frame wire

Gold strip

Mat

Glass

Backing board

Photograph

1 Arrange your photographs into a composition: ensure that none looks outward or away from the group. In our collection, we had four photographs of the same size and one smaller one. It was decided to put the small one in the center and range the others around it.

2 Use a piece of stiff cardboard — as here — or hardboard to provide a backing. For the mat itself, use mat card. Here, an ivory color was chosen to give an off-white, subdued paleness, onto which decorative lines could be drawn.

3 Backing board, mat and glass must all be the same size. If you wish to re-use an old frame, measure the height and width of the space within the frame, including the rabbet overlap, while the frame is upside down, and cut the board, mat and glass so that they fit snugly into it. Otherwise, determine the size of the mat first, as we have done here, and then cut the frame and mat. Cut the board with a craft knife.

4 Decide where to place the photographs, using your own judgment, but leaving more space at the bottom of the photographs than at the top, so that they sit up high in the mat; we have placed the middle photograph with 6 inches of space above it and 9 inches of space below.

5 Measure each photograph. Subtract about ½ inch from both the height and width measurements to allow for an overlapping margin of mat card — the photo will fit beneath the mat and must be slightly larger than the window, otherwise it will fall out. Lay the mat card flat and measure out the windows. If you are cutting by hand, rule lightly penciled lines on the front of the mat card before cutting.

7 When cutting the windows, use a straight-edge with a beveled slope and a rubber tread on the bottom to prevent it from slipping. Lay the straight-edge along the penciled line on the front of the mat card. Place a craft-knife blade at the top of one line and score a light cut, holding the blade against the beveled edge to give a sloped window. Run the blade along the line a second or third time until you have cut right through the card. Repeat this process until you have cut out all the windows.

6 Before cutting, check the right angles at the corners of the windows, using a protractor or try square.

8 Now stick down the photographs. Turn the mat card upside down and lay it flat. Place one photograph face downward onto its window and stick a piece of tape along one edge of the back of the photograph. Then turn the mat card over to check that the photograph is correctly positioned.

9 Once you are satisfied that the photograph is properly in place, turn the mat card face down again, and apply tape to the other sides of the photograph to secure it. Repeat this procedure with the other photographs.

10 Make one final check with all the photographs in place. Notice the final effect, here, of placing the photographs so that they sit high up in the mat-space. The outside photographs have a 2 inches space above them but a 3 inches space below them; and they are arranged symmetrically, with a ½ inch space between each, and a 3 inch space between them and the middle photograph, and a uniform distance from the sides of the mat.

11 Using an ordinary clear ruler, draw light lines with a sharp, hard pencil to mark where the decorative lines will fall. Check the right angles with a try square or protractor. It is up to you where you place the lines but avoid spacing them too evenly as this gives a dull effect. We decided to draw three lines around each photograph, one ¼ inch from the edge of the photograph, one ⅛ inch beyond that and a third ⅝ inch beyond that.

12 We used brown sepia ink for the two inner lines and gold ink for the outer one, drawing the lines with a lining pen. Place the rule upside down to avoid smudging the ink. Run the pen along the penciled line slowly and continuously. Felt-tipped pens can also be used for the lines.

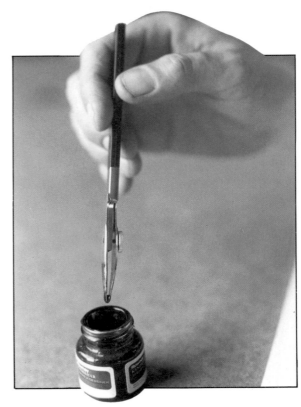

13 For the frame, we used a rabbeted frame molding, cut into four pieces and mitered. Before joining, we stained the pieces with middle oak color, using a rag to spread the stain. After joining, the frame was polished with clear wax.

14 Lengths of gold slip add a final touch to the framing. Place a piece along the inside of the back of the frame and measure it by eye, marking it off so that it fits tightly into the rabbet. Then miter the pieces.

15 Turn the frame upside down. Fit the gold slip snugly into place into the rabbet; next fit the glass; then the mat card with the photos; and finally the backing board. Tap 1 inch steel tacks into the frame at an angle so that they hold everything in place against the rabbet. There is no need to make holes first with a bradawl as the tacks are extremely sharp.

16 Tape the back along the edges with adhesive paper to keep out the dust. Finally, screw in two brass screw-eyes into the back of the molding, one on each side, a third of the way down the artpiece; run wire through from one side to the other and knot firmly.

PROJECT 5

Framing a manuscript

1 Purchase a length of ordinary builders' molding. Professionals may cut a rabbet into this with a rabbet plane but for this project a strip of quarter round was attached to the molding to make a rabbet.

Manuscripts usually have a serious, gray appearance. They can be brightened up considerably in the framing, without losing their dignity. We decided to use a triple mat for this manuscript, with a red slip included to give a touch of color. We cut the mats and windows first in the usual way.

Materials and equipment

Mat card (red and two tones of gray)	Miter box
	Saw
Hard, sharp pencil	Brads, 1 inch long
Ruler	Pigments and shellac
Scalpel or craft knife	Pewter wax
Pine builders' molding	Polishing rag
Quarter round	Brown paper tape
Woodwork glue	Bradawl
Nails	Screw-eyes
Hammer	Wire for wall-hanging
General purpose brush	Pliers
Vice or corner clamps	

2 Glue the quarter round to the molding. For extra strength, nail the two pieces together. Cut the finished length into four pieces and miter in the normal way.

Quarter round (forming rabbet)

Mats

Manuscript

Glass

Molding

Backing board

3 As an alternative to corner clamps, a vice can be used for making a main frame. Place one piece of quarter round and molding firmly in the vice, and apply glue to the end.

5 Check that the glued pieces are held firmly in the vice before nailing the corners. Then hammer in a 1 inch brad. One brad in each corner should suffice.

4 Adjust the vice to hold another piece against the glued strip. Make a hole ready for a nail, using a bradawl. Hand-held pressure is enough, as this is a piece of soft pine.

7 We applied a blue-black undercoat, using pigment mixed with shellac. We left a groove in this darker color to add decorative interest and gave the rest of the frame a pewter wax finish. Ready-made waxes are available in different colors. Apply either with a brush or with the finger. Wait for a few days before polishing, or you will rub off the wax.

8 Assemble the glass, mat, manuscript and backing board and tap nails into the inside edges of the frame to hold the component parts together. Place brown paper tape on the back to keep out the dust and attach screw-eyes and wire in the usual way for hanging.

6 When the whole frame has been glued and nailed together, make sure that the mats fit properly. Assemble the mats to check, and trim them if necessary. Remove the manuscript and mats, so that the frame can be decorated.

Framing a piece of needlework

1 A length of molding is used for the inner, velvet-covered insert, or slip frame. Make sure that the rabbet is deeper than the depth of the stretcher, so that the stretcher will eventually fit right down into the slip frame. Cut and miter the wood, then spray the pieces with fabric glue.

N eedlework is often attached to a stretcher before being framed to give it an extra smartness and tautness. Place the needlework over a stretcher similar to that used for an oil painting, and staple it round the edges.

We framed this piece of embroidery under glass, and it was decided to keep it from contact with the glass in an elegant way by putting a velvet slip frame between the embroidery and the glass.

Materials and equipment

Wood strips for stretcher	Mahogany molding with
Hammer	rabbet
Stapler for stretcher	Woodwork glue
Molding with rabbet	Corner clamps
Hard, sharp pencil	Glass, 1/12 inch thick
Ruler	Bradawl
Miter box	Nails
Saw	Brads
Fabric glue	Screw-eyes for wall-
Velvet	hanging
Scalpel or craft knife	Wire for wall-hanging

2 With a scalpel cut pieces of velvet large enough to cover the rabbet, and front and side of the insert. Wrap each piece of velvet round a glued piece of insert and press firmly.

Embroidery on stretcher

Main frame

Velvet-covered slip frame

Glass

4 A length of mahogany molding was chosen for the main frame. This outer frame, of course, must be deeper than the insert. Cut and miter the molding so that the insert will fit snugly into the frame.

5 The clamp we used consists of four metal corners. The fourth corner has a screw-tightener attached to it and a piece of wire leading from it.

3 Make sure that the velvet covers the insert and rabbet except at the back, so that only the velvet will show when the insert is fitted into the main frame. With a scalpel, trim off all the excess velvet from the edges and corners.

6 Apply glue to the mitered ends of the molding, and stick together. Fit the corners of the Elwood clamp onto the corners of the frame and run the wire around the whole frame, making sure that it sits in the grooves provided for it in the metal corners. Then fasten the wire in the screw-tightener and tighten it up just enough to ensure that the glued corners will be stuck firmly. Wait for the glue to dry and then nail the corners. Make the slip frame in the same way.

7 The components are now ready for assembly. Lay the main frame face down. Fit a piece of glass into its rabbet and then fit the slip frame into the back of the main frame.

9 Hammer nails into the holes which you have made in the inside edges of the main frame. Use sharp brads to ensure that you can tap them into place without using too much force.

10 Now take the needlework on its stretcher and place it in the rabbet of the slip frame. Tap nails into the inside edges of the slip frame to hold the stretcher in place.

11 The frame is now complete. The needlework is protected from dirt and dust by the glass, and protected from direct contact with the glass by the velvet-covered slip frame. A treasured piece of embroidery can be neatly preserved in this way.

8 Next, secure the slip frame in the outer frame. Make the holes in the outer main frame with a bradawl, one in each side. Remember that you will be doing this with the glass already in place and the slip frame behind it, so work in the bradawl gently.

PROJECT 7

Framing the three-dimensional

The butterflies to be framed were fixed with pins to cork bases, making framing a tricky, delicate affair. For instance, velvet was chosen for the background: should the cork bases be glued onto velvet? Glue could damage such a delicate material.

Black velvet was chosen to off-set the butterflies, an effect which could easily be ruined by dust. So a dust-free working environment was essential and care had to be taken to make the finished frame tight and secure.

Materials and Equipment

Box molding, 2 inches deep, 3/4 inch wide	Ruler
	Corner clamps
	Counter-sinker (optional)
Glass, 1/12 inch thick	Bradawl
Sharp, hard pencil	Brass screws
Length of wooden quarter round	Screwdriver
	Black mat paint
Woodwork glue	Craft knife or scalpel
Hand drill	Black velvet
Brads, 5/8 inch	Hardboard
Hammer	Fabric glue
Punch	Screws, 5/8 inch
Dark woodstain	Brown paper tape
Miter box	Brass plates and screws
Saw	

1 Choose a piece of molding deep enough to ensure that a space large enough to accommodate the items to be framed exists between the glass and the back of the frame. We chose a piece of boxmolding 2 inches deep and 3/4 inch thick. Hold the glass along the edge of the rabbet, and mark its precise thickness along the molding with a pencil.

2 Select a piece of quarter round. This will be stuck along the inside of the rabbet to create a groove in which the glass will be fitted. Make sure the quarter round is not so deep that it will be visible behind the glass.

Hardboard base

Quarter round (forming rabbet)

Glass

Frame/box surround

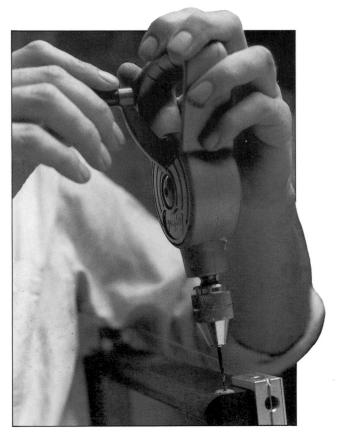

3 Place the length of quarter round along the molding, and glue it in place over the penciled line. Apply tape to give it extra temporary strength. Once the glue has set, drill small holes through the quarter round into the main frame and hammer $5/8$ inch brads into it. Punch them beneath the wood surface for a neat effect.

6 The final side of the frame is not glued or nailed, but screwed on, so that it can be removed if the glass ever needs replacing. Holding the frame steady with a clamp, drill into the corners.

4 Stain the molding and quarter round with a dark woodstain, and cut it into four pieces, mitering the corners in the usual way. Join two short sides and one long side of the frame to allow the glass to be fitted into the groove.

5 After gluing and nailing the three sides of the frame together, carefully slide the sheet of glass into place in the groove.

7 It is often a good idea to use a counter-sinker for fine-finish work of this type. By making tiny 'craters' at the entrance of the drilled holes, the screws will not jut out above the surface of the wood. Make sure you do not over-do this.

8 Carefully screw brass screws into the holes, resting them snugly in the hollow, to give a professional look.

9 Paint the inside of the frame black. The use of a matt black will match, but not overwhelm, the black velvet that will provide a matting base for the group of butterflies.

10 Measure out a piece of hardboard to the same size as the frame and stick the piece of black velvet onto it with fabric glue. Cut out the piece of hardboard.

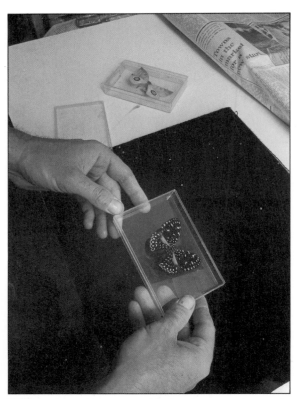

11 Decide where you wish to place each specimen and measure out their positions on the back of the hardboard.

12 As the slightest spilling of glue could damage the velvet, we decided to screw the cork bases in place in this project. This is why it was important to plot the positions of the butterflies on the back.

13 Using $^5/_8$ inch screws, carefully screw through the back of the hardboard, so that the screws protrude through the front. The cork bases of the butterflies are then carefully screwed onto the threads of the screws.

14 Place the hardboard and specimens onto the back of the frame. Make holes with a bradawl, drill and then fix a screw into each corner to provide a firm attachment.

15 Tape over the hardboard with brown paper tape to make absolutely sure no dust can get in. Finally, fit brass plates to the sides of the frame so that it can be screwed flat onto a wall.

PROJECT 8

Restoring a gilded frame

1 Some of the ornamentation in this frame has cracked badly and some has been completely lost. There is extensive damage to one corner of the frame, and two sides need general repair.

This mid-nineteenth century wooden frame, gilded and beautifully embellished with intricate ornamentation, is sadly in need of repair. With skill and patience and some common materials, one of which is widely used by dentists, the frame can be brought back vividly to life.

2 Much can be achieved by cleaning with soap and water. Be careful not to use too much water as this can damage the frame. After cleaning off the surface grease and dust, lightly brush over with acetone, a chemical cleaner used for gold leaf.

Materials and equipment

Soap, water, rag	Woodwork glue
Acetone cleaner	Sandpaper
Brush	Gesso
Vaseline	Bole
Alginate mold solution	Gold leaf
Knife (for spreading)	Lacquer
Cooking oil or grease	Staining wax
Plaster	Container such as a tin
Plaster spatula or carving tool	lid

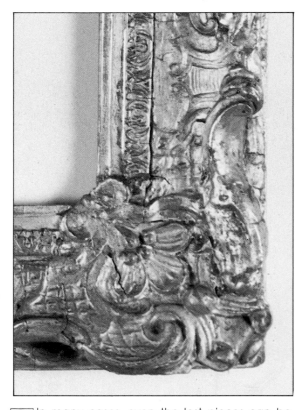

3 In many cases, even the lost pieces can be "recovered" by taking molds from the good fragments that remain. Search the frame for areas of ornamentation still in good condition.

4 Apply Vaseline with a brush, working thoroughly into all the areas from which you intend to take molds. This will prevent the molding material from sticking to the wood.

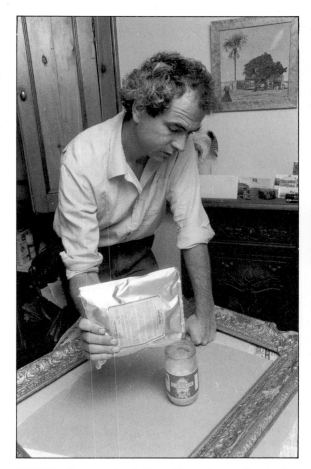

5 Mix the mold solution. Alginate, similar to the substance dentists use to make molds for crowns, can be obtained from dental suppliers or from general mold suppliers, such as model shops. It gives a very high definition, and is very useful for molding intricate embellishments.

6 While the mold is still in a semi-liquid state, apply it to the required spot. Press it into crevices and corners with a knife, working quickly, as it sets in a matter of minutes.

7 Cover all the areas from which you intend to make molds, and leave for a few minutes to allow it to dry and set. Apply a generous coating so that each mold will be strong and substantial when removed.

8 When they are set, peel off the molds carefully. They will have a rubbery, flexible texture, but will tear quite easily. Also note that molds made from alginate do not last very long.

9 Apply cooking oil or grease to the molds so that the plaster will not stick to them. Select a plaster. Press the plaster paste into the mold and leave it for a few hours to set. Apply glue to the damaged areas and then press the plaster firmly into place. Some minor alterations may need to be made; use a plaster spatula or carving tools for these finishing touches. Then rub down lightly with sandpaper.

10 Apply two or three coats of gesso to the plaster to provide a base for the gold leaf. Rub down with fine sandpaper. Then apply two coats of bole coloring, a dark, terracotta reddish-brown, allowing time for drying in between applications.

11 Apply gold leaf in the usual way. Lacquer the gold leaf with a hot colorless type of lacquer, to provide protection. You will notice that the repaired sections of the frame look much newer than the rest of the frame. It is therefore necessary to tone down the new parts so that they blend with the rest. Waxes and pigments can be used for this.

12 Mix the staining wax and pigment in a shallow container; a tin lid is used here. A variety of waxes are available. We chose staining waxes with brown and black coloring.

13 Apply successive layers of wax with a rag, until the right color is achieved. As an alternative to staining waxes, water and pigments can be used and then waxed afterward.

14 You may have to work in several layers of wax before you are satisfied that the new areas blend with the original. The result will be a richly decorated frame, with the craftsmanship of an earlier era restored to perfection.

Care and repair

real gold leaf — if your frame is a particularly fine one — to simpler and quicker retouching. Sometimes it is just the glass which needs replacing and this is an easier task.

Although it is best to leave valuable works to the professional, there are some basic techniques which, once mastered, will enable you to carry out many minor repairs to give a surprisingly new look to pictures and frames.

REPAIRING OLD FRAMES

It is important to be cautious when renovating old frames and if in doubt give the job to a professional.

Most of the frames bought from antique stores are nineteenth- and early twentieth-century reproductions. While these are not particularly valuable, they are well-made frames, more individual and interesting then many modern moldings, and well worth reviving, as they will probably last for many more years.

Many such frames have some kind of gold finish. Some are basic wooden frames with plaster moldings and gilded finishes; others are carved wooden frames decorated in gold leaf; and others are gold-painted wooden frames.

When cleaning gold leaf, there is one important 'don't' to remember: never harshly rub or wash it with water, as this action wipes off much of the actual gold surface, a veneer so delicate that it is all too easy to damage. Instead, carefully wipe the gold leaf with a diluted bleach solution or acetone; or brighten the gold with lemon, rubbing a slice of lemon gently over the molding.

Repairing Chipped Gilt

The easiest way to repair small chips in gilt is to touch up the damaged spot with gilt paste, which is available in art and craft stores, or, if very small, with gold paint. However, if a small portion of the molding is missing, it might be necessary to fill in the missing area with plastic wood, barbola paste, putty or

A central part of picture framing is the care and repair of the frames. Apart from looking after your own frames, you may wish to detach an attractive old frame from an unsuitable picture and give it a new lease of life. Or you may have an old print or picture that needs attention before it can be placed in a frame. Consequently, we have also included in this section some tips on simple picture cleaning and restoring.

If you do buy an old frame, first be careful to ensure that you are not spoiling a rare antique by attempting to renovate it. Your local antique store should be able to advise you on this. If you have bought an old frame without antique value in itself, then you can achieve a great deal by cleaning and renovating it. For instance, if an old molded plaster frame is damaged in places, it is usually well worth-while repairing these dents and chips by taking a mold from the good parts of the frame and using this to build up the damaged parts with filler. There are different ways of renovating gilding, from using

Replacing decorations
Badly damaged or chipped frames can often be repaired by making plaster replacements for the damaged parts from molds taken from good portions of the frame. If a frame still has a good corner, for instance, a whole corner piece can be recreated in this way (right).

Chipped gilt frames
The gilded frames (left and below) are both slightly chipped. Such chips can be repaired by casting plaster replacements from molds. Alternatively, very small areas can sometimes be built up by hand and touched up with gold paint. The gold slip frame (far left) is held in place by wooden wedges — a device often used in older frames.

Second hand frames
This frame (right) was bought second hand, in poor condition. The gesso and gilt were chipped and the corners were worn and loose. The frame was first thoroughly cleaned and then dismantled. The corners were then re-mitered, so that the frame fitted the new painting precisely.

Damaged frame
The gilded frame around this landscape print (right) *is faded and badly damaged. The chipped, damaged corners* (above) *could be touched up but in this case the framer decided to remove the gesso and gilt completely by soaking and scrubbing. Many such old frames have solid and attractive wooden bases that can be cleaned and polished.*

speckling compound. Such a filler can be molded into shape with a paintbrush handle or fine sculpting tool to blend it in with the original. When the area is dry, it can be matched to the original with the gilt paste.

Of course, gold leaf itself can be used to repair original gold leaf surfaces. However, this is rarely advisable as new gold leaf shines brightly and will look out of place on a more mellowed gold leaf frame. All gilt repairs tend to suffer to a certian extent from this problem but there are a few ways of getting round it. One way is to make use of the antiquing technique described on page 92. Another is to age the new gilt instantly: rub tiny amounts of adhesive onto the newly renovated molding and sprinkle a little dust onto the area. Wipe away the loose dust and you are left with a perfect older-looking frame.

Larger Repairs

If an area of wooden or plaster molding is missing that is too large or too intricate to build up with filler materials, it is sometimes worth making your own mold for the missing portion. This is usually not too difficult as many of the frames requiring this treatment were themselves originally manufactured from molds. *(See pages 128–131 for further details.)*

Use a piece of the frame which is intact and undamaged as the base for your mold. Press Plasticine onto this area of the frame to obtain an impression of the pattern. Remove from the frame and build up the edges of the Plasticine mold with more Plasticine. Then pour in plaster of Paris up to the depth required to fit into the missing section. When dry,

remove the dried plaster molding from the Plasticine and glue it into place.

Although Plasticine is easily available from department stores, many modern picture framers use alternative substances, such as silicone rubber and an organic material based on seaweed called Alginate, which can be obtained from specialist stores. The organic material and the silicone rubber give very precise impressions but Alginate lasts only a few days once the mold has been made, so is not suitable for long-term projects.

Stripping Old Frames

Some old plaster frames are beyond repair and may not be to your taste in any case. Do not throw these away, however, as most old plaster moldings were created on very well made wooden bases, often pine, which make excellent frames in their own right. Remove the plaster by immersing the frames in hot water and scrubbing. When the stripped frame is dry, finely sandpaper it and then wax or stain it to produce a solid, new-look frame.

REPLACING GLASS

Often what seems to be a dingy or yellowed picture is in fact a clean picture languishing behind a dirty, aging, nicotine-stained piece of old glass. Very old-fashioned glass often distorts a picture. Sometimes the glass can be removed and washed; sometimes it needs replacing.

To dismantle a frame, place the picture face down on a clean, soft surface. Then gently remove the tacks which hold the backing and the picture in place. Lift up the picture and remove the glass.

Renovating oil paintings

Surface Dirt

It is a mistake to assume that your rather gloomy-looking oil painting is necessarily a dirty one. Many such paintings were intended to look dark: portraits and still-lifes, for instance, were traditionally given a dark background in the eighteenth and nineteenth centuries, and many landscape painters used a great deal of brown in their trees and grass. Many paintings look dark because of the mastic varnish covering them. This type of varnish, widely used until twenty years ago, has a dulling effect on paintings that is now familiar — the yellowing skies, brown foliage, and general dinginess often seen on pictures found in attics, junk stores and the more neglected museums.

However, many paintings are simply dirty and there are some basic steps which can be taken to improve them before reframing them. Surface dirt, accumulated through years of exposure to dust, nicotine, oil lamps and open fires is relatively easy to remove without damaging the picture (although it is not advisable to do even this much on a picture of high value). Wipe the surface of the old painting with cotton batting soaked in paint thinner. The older the varnish, the safer this method is: if a picture has been varnished recently, the paint thinner will tend to dissolve the varnish as well. By removing the surface grime in this way, the colors of the painting can be appreciably brightened.

You may find that a painting has not been varnished at all and that dirt is engrained into the paint. If this is the case you will need to wipe the painting with cotton batting soaked in a weak solution of amonia to remove the dirt. However, by using amonia you do run the risk of removing the paint as well as the dirt, so do not attempt it on any paintings that are valuable to you.

Removing Old Varnish

Extreme caution is required when removing a coat of old varnish from a painting. Tackle a small area at a time, using a solvent such as acetone, methyl alcohol or ethyl alcohol; if the varnish is fairly new, paint thinner might be sufficient. Starting with the darker areas, apply the solvent cautiously with swabs of cotton batting. It is better to leave fragments of old varnish, which will not necessarily be noticed, than to be so anxious to remove every scrap of old varnish that you also remove a crucial detail of the painting.

Dealing with Flaking Paint

The professional will go to great lengths to recover flakes of paint that are missing from a painting. This is not so ridiculous as it sounds, especially if the painting has been behind glass, since the missing flakes will be stuck somewhere in the frame. Once discovered, the restorer will patiently fit the flakes back into the picture as though completing a jigsaw puzzle. The pieces are stuck into place with beeswax, which has a very low melting point. The beeswax is placed on the appropriate spot in the picture and the flake of paint positioned on top of this. Then a heated spatula — a very fine one — is applied on top of the flake, so that the beeswax beneath melts and the flake can be precisely maneuvered into position. Although this is a specialist technique, there is no reason why the home renovator cannot become

adept at it, using a heated teaspoon handle instead of a spatula if need be.

If the missing flakes of paint are irretrievably lost and you do not wish to hand the painting over to an expert, you might wish to paint over the problem areas.

Sometimes, a fine portion of missing paint will have left an uneven picture surface. An indentation can be built up very carefully, using speckling compound or even putty and, in the case of a very slight indentation, a thicker layer of paint may well suffice.

Use either oils or acrylics to paint over the problem spots of the picture. These areas will often be white: where the top paint has flaked off, the white primer — the "undercoat" which is applied to the canvas before the oil paint — usually remains. The advantage of using acrylic paint, especially if it is to be applied thickly, is that it dries very quickly; the equivalent amount of oil paint can sometimes take weeks to dry.

If you are not used to painting, remember that you must match the tone as well as the color. For instance, a red jacket may not be red in the simple sense but might actually be a more dingy color and contain more gray than red. It is advisable to tone down your colors with a neutral pigment, such as raw umber or Payne's gray, and experiment on a separate piece of paper until you obtain exactly the right shade.

Cracks in the Paint

Almost all old paintings have surface cracks, which actually serve to authenticate the picture. By studying the distance between the cracks and identifying the types of cracks that they are, an expert can "read" a painting, that is, identify when the painting was originally executed. Experts suspect a fake if they can find no cracks, or if the signature contains no cracks, and if one area of a painting is without

135

Renovating prints, watercolors, maps and documents

cracks it has probably been repaired.

Therefore, unless the cracks in your old oil painting are really disfiguring, it is best to leave them alone.

Revarnishing
Either mat or semi-gloss varnish can be coated onto an old painting, although a very high-gloss varnish will look unnatural. Dilute the varnish to two parts varnish and one part paint thinner and apply it with a brush vertically, then horizontally, using even, parallel strokes to achieve a smooth coat. Avoid applying thick coats of varnish as this will make the picture look as if it has been encapsulated in plastic.

Alternatively, use a spray can of varnish; this is preferable, as an aerosol gives a more even application than a brush. Nevertheless, the varnish must still be sprayed in thin, light coats: hold the picture upright and spray it from about 1 foot away, avoiding a build-up of varnish in any one area, which would probably drip.

Whichever method you use, it is absolutely essential that you work in clean, dust-free surroundings. If any particles of fluff or dirt become stuck in the varnish, they will look prominent and unsightly.

An old print
This print (right) is typical of many that you will come across. It is badly damaged and in need of flattening as well as cleaning.

Making the canvas taut
Purpose-built stretchers have corner wedges which can be tapped in gently (above). This pushes the sides apart and tightens the canvas.

Tightening the Canvas
Tightening a canvas that has become loose is a simple task. In many cases, professionally made canvases can be made taut again without having to remove the tacks that join the canvas to the stretcher. If you turn the canvas over, you will usually find that the corners of the stretcher have been slotted together and held slightly apart by tiny wedges of wood to provide the original final tightening of the canvas. A gentle tap will drive these wedges inward slighly and provide a new tautness for the canvas.

Many prints and watercolors become damp over the years and, like oil paintings, their surface can become dingy with dust. Because prints and watercolors are usually executed on paper, they are also subject to staining, mildew and buckling. They can be ripped and scratched, too.

Removing Surface Dirt
Removing grime from a dingy surface, often the result of the print not having been behind glass, is not simply a case of giving the surface a quick wipe, as it can be sometimes with oil paintings. Because the paper on which the painting was done is porous, the grime will have been absorbed to a certain extent. Removing dirt from the picture surface, therefore, is a job for an expert. However, the white areas

around and within the picture can sometimes be dealt with by the home renovator — and this can often be enough to give the whole picture a facelift. Wipe gently over the white areas with a putty eraser. Alternatively, wipe the whole surface with carbon tetrachloride — a dry-cleaning solution available from drugstores. This must be wiped evenly all over the picture, including the image area, to avoid a blotchy result.

Dealing with Creases

Creases can sometimes be removed by sandwiching the canvas between two sheets of blotting paper and keeping it under a heavy, even weight for several days. If this does not work, it may be necessary to stretch the paper. Immerse the picture in cold water for just long enough to wet the paper (the water will not make the watercolors run as long as the whole print is immersed). Then place the picture on a flat surface and stick it down with brown paper tape. Allow the picture to dry naturally — artificial drying makes the paper contract too quickly and tear. Remove the tape to leave a completely flat picture.

Removing Damp Stains and Foxing

Damp stains and the little spots of mildew known as foxing can be removed by bleaching. Do not use ordinary commerical bleach; one per cent standardized sodium hypochlorite solution is suitable — the solution used for sterilizing babies' bottles, obtainable from drugstores. Mix it in a ratio of one part solution to three parts cold water and put it into a flat photographers' tray or baking dish. Immerse the print or watercolor in the solution for a few minutes until the blemishes start to disappear. As soon as the dark spots begin to fade, remove the print and place it in a bath of water for a few minutes to wash away the bleaching solution. After rinsing, you may well need to stretch the canvas, especially if the watercolor is on light- to medium-weight paper. Partially dry the canvas naturally, then place it between two sheets of clean, dry blotting paper to finish off the drying. The marks should by now have disappeared.

Covering Scratches

Retouching a scratched area is generally a professional job. However, if you do decide to embark on this, begin with a paint that is more diluted than usual and gradually build up the

The problem of mold
This print (above) is marred by mold. Most engravings will withstand washing and, sometimes, bleaching. Here, an oxidizing agent will be used to remove the stains and improve overall appearance.

intensity of the color. When repairing tears, it is important to lay the surfaces together without disturbing the fibres in the paper, which means that you must find their original positions and piece them back together before gluing them into place.

TEARS

Small tears, where there is sufficient overlap, can usually be repaired by applying acid-free, colorless adhesive that does not shrink as it dries. To repair large tears, however, you will probably need to fix thin backing paper to the back of the picture, so that no gap is visible.

Damaged engraving
Varnish, applied to give the appearance of an oil painting, has darkened with age on this hand-colored print (left). A solvent was needed to remove ingrained varnish deposits.

Glossary

Abstract expressionism
An art form in which expression of the artist's inner experience is more important than realism. Paintings are created from involuntary marks and dribbles of paint.

Acrylic
Tough, inflexible type of plastic available in sheet form and sometimes used in framing instead of glass.

Acrylic paint
A comparatively new paint in which the pigment is suspended in a synthetic resin.

Ancien Régime
The period in Europe before the French Revolution.

Baroque
The richly decorative style of the post-Renaissance, prevalent in Europe in the seventeenth and eighteenth centuries.

Bevel
The rounded or sloped edge of a ruler or strip of wood, or the sloped inside edge of a window in a mat.

Block mat
A block of wood or particle board onto which a print or other picture is matted.

Builders' molding
Strips of wood used by builders for trimming doors, windows, base boards etc, which can be used to make picture frames.

Clip frame
A simple frame without an edge or surround, formed by clipping a sheet of glass to a wooden backing.

Cold matting
See Wet matting.

Composition
The arrangement of the elements that make up the content of a picture.

Conservation matting
Matting carried out with acid-free materials to preserve old or valuable documents and pictures.

Damask
A fabric woven with a pattern which is visible on both sides.

Dry matting
A method of sticking a picture onto a backing. A sheet of film is placed between the two and heat is applied. The film dissolves, fusing the picture and backing. Also known as hot matting.

Emery
Cloth or paper covered with emery powder, for sanding a fine finish.

Empire style
The fashion associated with Napoleonic France, in the late eighteenth and early nineteenth centuries.

Foxing
Tiny spots of mildew that can form on old prints and drawings.

Framers' molding
Strips of rabbeted wood especially designed for picture frames.

Fresco
Painting carried out on mortar or plaster that is not quite dry.

Gesso
Prepared surface of plaster as a ground for gilding and other finishes.

Gilding
Applying a gold finish.

Glaze
(1) To cover with glass, as with glass in a frame. (2) A thin coat of a transparent color that is placed over a differently colored undercoat.

Gold leaf
Thin sheets of beaten gold which can be applied to frames.

Hinge mat
A mat which opens and closes on a hinge, enabling the picture to be positioned and removed easily.

Hot matting
See Dry matting.

Insert
A smaller frame within the outer frame. Sometimes referred to as a slip frame.

Mastic
Natural gum from which some paints and varnishes are made.

Mat
The card which is used as a backing for a flimsy picture, and the card from which a window is cut, beneath which a picture is placed.

Memorabilia
Articles and ephemera that have nostalgic associations.

Miter
The 45-degree angled cut, made in the ends of each side of the frame.

Modernism
Art styles pertaining to and identifying with the twentieth century.

Neoclassical revival
Art movements of the eighteenth and nineteenth centuries that looked back to classical, ie Greek and Roman, times.

Neutral
Without positive or distinctive characteristics.

Particle board
Rigid board made from compressed chips of wood.

Patina
A finish often used as a base for glazes or to modify and tone a color.

Quarter round
Strip of wood or metal, shaped like a quarter-circle, often used to form a rabbet.

Rabbet
The L-shaped groove on the reverse side of framers' molding into which the glass, mat, artpiece and backing board fit.

Sampler
Piece of embroidery worked in a variety of stitches, which was traditionally worked to demonstrate accomplishment in needlework.

Score
To cut, in glass or card, a line that does not pass through the material completely.

Sepia
A rich brown pigment obtained from cuttle fish. Now used to describe the color only.

Slip frame
An inner frame, usually covered in fabric, inserted between the main frame and picture to provide a decorative border in the same way as a mat. Also known as an insert.

Stretcher
An expandable wooden frame to which a canvas is usually tacked before framing, so that it can be made taut in the frame.

Transfer gold or silver
Thin sheets of beaten gold or silver attached to paper and rubbed onto the surface of a frame.

Veneer
A thin layer or inlay of flat wood applied to a surface.

Vignette
A picture or design, usually done on a small scale, without a boundary.

Wash
Thinly diluted paint used to obtain a transparent or delicate paint finish.

Wet matting
A method of sticking a picture to a backing, using spray glue or wallpaper size. Also known as cold matting.

Wood strip
Narrow strip of wood, sometimes used to frame an artpiece.

Index

Page numbers in *italic* refer to illustrations and captions

Acknowledgments

The pictures on these pages were produced by courtesy of the following:

8 Scrovegni, Padua; **9** National Gallery, London (t,b); **10** National Portrait Gallery, London; **11** Private collection, London; **14** Private collection, London (tr,br); **15** Private collection, London (t,b); **16** Private collection, London (bl,cr); **17** Private collection, London; **18** Private collection, London (t); **19** Private collection, London (r); **20** Private collection, London (tl,bl,br); **23** Private collection, London (t,b); **24** Elizabeth Whiting & Associates; **25** Elizabeth Whiting & Associates; **26** Elizabeth Whiting & Associates (tl,bl,tr,br); **27** Elizabeth Whiting & Associates (t,b); **28** Elizabeth Whiting & Associates; **29** Elizabeth Whiting & Associates (t); **31** Stan Smith (t), Rosie Waites (b); **34** *The World of Interiors*, photograph – John Cook; **35** Trustees of the British Museum, London (t); **39** *The World of Interiors*, photograph – John Cook; **42** *The World of Interiors*, photograph – John Cook; **43** *The World of Interiors*, photograph – John Cook; **136** Victoria and Albert Museum, London (br); **137** Victoria and Albert Museum, London (bl,tr).

With special thanks to Patricia Monahan and John Shrimpton.

All other photographs are the property of Quarto Publishing Ltd.

Key: (t) top; (b) bottom; (l) left; (r) right; (c) center

While every effort has been made to acknowledge all copyright holders, we apologize if any omissions have been made.